WORLD HISTORY
THE HUMAN EXPERIENCE

History Simulations

NATIONAL GEOGRAPHIC SOCIETY

Mounir A. Farah

Andrea Berens Karls

GLENCOE
McGraw-Hill

New York, New York   Columbus, Ohio   Woodland Hills, California   Peoria, Illinois

Customize Your Resources

No matter how you organize your teaching resources, Glencoe has what you need.

The **Teacher's Classroom Resources** for *World History: The Human Experience* provides you with a wide variety of supplemental materials to enhance the classroom experience. These resources appear as individual booklets accompanied by a file management kit of file folders, labels, and tabbed binder dividers in a carryall file box. The booklets are designed to open flat so that pages can be easily photocopied without removing them from their booklets. However, if you choose to create separate files, the pages are perforated for easy removal. You may customize these materials using our file folders or tabbed dividers.

The individual booklets and the file management kit supplied in **Teacher's Classroom Resources** give you the flexibility to organize these resources in a combination that best suits your teaching style. Below are several alternatives:

- **Organize all resources by category**
  (all Tests, all Geography and History Activities, all History Simulations, and so on, filed separately)

- **Organize resources by category and chapter**
  (all Chapter 1 activities, all Chapter 1 tests, etc.)

- **Organize resources sequentially by lesson**
  (activities, quizzes, study guides, etc., for Section 1, Section 2, and so on)

Glencoe/McGraw-Hill
A Division of The McGraw·Hill Companies

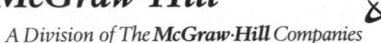

Copyright © by the McGraw-Hill Companies, Inc. All rights reserved. Permission is granted to reproduce the material contained herein on the condition that such material be reproduced only for classroom use; be provided to students, teachers, and families without charge; and be used solely in conjunction with *World History: The Human Experience*. Any other reproduction, for use or sale, is prohibited without prior written permission of the publisher.

Send all inquiries to:
Glencoe/McGraw-Hill
936 Eastwind Drive
Westerville, OH 43081

ISBN 0-02-823230-5

Printed in the United States of America
5 6 7 8 9   045   02 01 00 99

HISTORY SIMULATIONS

TABLE OF CONTENTS

To the Teacher ... iv

Chapter 1	Can You Dig It?	1
Chapter 2	Let's Get Acquainted	3
Chapter 3	Talking Heads	5
Chapter 4	Visiting History	7
Chapter 5	Playing Aristotle	9
Chapter 6	A Roman Mural	11
Chapter 7	Culture Quest	13
Chapter 8	Cast in Stone	15
Chapter 9	China Challenge	17
Chapter 10	Illumination	19
Chapter 11	Understanding Islam	21
Chapter 12	Meet the Medievals	23
Chapter 13	The Duties of the Pope	25
Chapter 14	Territorial Tracks	27
Chapter 15	Asking Around	29
Chapter 16	A Renaissance Fair	31
Chapter 17	The Search for Andronia	33
Chapter 18	Empire Bingo	35
Chapter 19	King or Queen for a Day	37
Chapter 20	The Educational Contract	39
Chapter 21	Unrest in Blaat	41
Chapter 22	Where Do They Stand?	43
Chapter 23	Pass It On!	45
Chapter 24	Through the Eyes of Artists	47
Chapter 25	Charting a Course . . . Again!	49
Chapter 26	Power Plays	51
Chapter 27	*The Imperial Press*	53
Chapter 28	In the Trenches	55
Chapter 29	The Postwar World	57
Chapter 30	What's My Name?	59
Chapter 31	The Path to War	61
Chapter 32	What Am I?	63
Chapter 33	Facts on Asia: A Cause-Effect Game	65
Chapter 34	Creating National Unity	67
Chapter 35	Give Peace a Chance	69
Chapter 36	Name That Leader	71
Chapter 37	Cash For Your Country	73

To the Teacher

History Simulations provide students with the opportunity to work in small groups to explore a theme, a topic, or a concept from *World History: The Human Experience.* Many of these activities use a game or simulation format to stimulate student interest.

The Teacher Material for each History Simulation lays out the learning objective and provides suggestions for teacher preparation. In addition, it contains detailed instructions to help clarify the tasks, which will enable the groups to work independently to meet the activity goals.

The second page of every History Simulation is a handout page designed to help groups document their efforts by filling out a chart, diagram, or planning sheet. Students will work in small groups in which all members have individual accountability and work together toward a common goal. *History Simulations* will help them to master the skills they need to work effectively in a group.

History Simulation 1

Can You Dig It?

Much of what we know about prehistory is the result of the work of archaeologists who unearth and interpret the artifacts left behind by prehistoric people. Both skill and luck are necessary to identify the best archaeological sites and find artifacts. Then the archaeologists must face the difficult task of making inferences from these remains about prehistoric life.

TEACHER MATERIAL

Learning Objective To demonstrate how archaeologists make inferences about prehistoric people from artifacts.

Activity Students simulate discovering an archaeological site and drawing inferences about the people who lived there from descriptions of artifacts found at the site.

Teacher Preparation Make one copy of the Handout Material on page 2 for each group. Label ten small brown paper bags from 1 to 10 and pin them to different locations on a wall map of the world. Have more bags than groups of students.

Activity Guidelines

1. Review with students the terms *archaeologist* and *artifact*. Ask students to suggest artifacts that might be found at an archeological site.

2. Tell students that they will "bury" artifacts at an archaeological site, discover the location of another archaeological site by a guessing game, and then infer information about a culture from the artifacts they "dig." The bags pinned on the map will simulate possible archaeological sites.

3. Organize the class into groups of four to five and give each group a worksheet. Have groups choose members to do the following tasks: write artifact clues to be "buried," participate in a guessing game, record the group's discussion of the artifacts found at the site it "digs," prepare a report, and give an oral presentation.

4. Each group uses the textbook to select one prehistoric group or early civilization, chooses the types of artifacts to describe, and writes clues for the chosen artifacts. For example, if a group chooses *Homo habilis,* it might describe (1) tool: stone—crudely finished with sharp edges; (2) weapon: part of a wooden club—roughly fashioned from a tree limb.

5. Each group puts its completed artifact clues into the numbered bag on the map that you designate. Be sure that the other groups do not observe which site is used.

6. Pair off the groups to play a guessing game. In a question-and-answer session, each group determines the map location of the other group's site by framing questions based on where the numbered bags are on the map; for example, "Is the site located south of the Equator?"

7. Have each group study the descriptions of the artifacts it "dug" and brainstorm inferences about the prehistoric group, using the guide on the worksheet to prompt discussion but also thinking of other considerations on their own. They then report to the class.

8. As each group reports, ask it to identify the culture whose artifacts it discovered. Ask the group that placed clues in a bag if the group that "dug" its site correctly identified the culture. You may use the following questions to summarize the activity:

   - What other information, if any, would have helped you make your inferences?
   - On what basis were your inferences made?
   - How did this activity give you a better understanding of the work of archaeologists?

Name .... Date .... Class ....

HISTORY SIMULATION 1

HANDOUT MATERIAL

Can You Dig It?—Creating an Archaeological Site

Choose a prehistoric group or early civilization from the text. Based on your selection, describe three or more artifacts. The artifacts can be chosen from the types listed below. When your descriptions are completed, cut them out and place them in the bag at the site your teacher designates.

- ☐ tools
- ☐ weapons
- ☐ clothing
- ☐ pottery
- ☐ burned wood
- ☐ jewelry
- ☐ art objects
- ☐ clay tablets with writing

Type of artifact _____	Type of artifact _____
Description _____	Description _____
_____	_____
_____	_____

Type of artifact _____	Type of artifact _____
Description _____	Description _____
_____	_____
_____	_____

Guide for Reporting on an Archaeological Site

To help your group start a discussion, consider the following categories when making inferences based on the artifacts you found at the archaeological site.

- Probable identity or function of each artifact
- Level of technological achievement
- Level of cultural advancement

Record your conclusions below. Be prepared to explain how you reached them.

_____

_____

_____

_____

HISTORY SIMULATION 2

Let's Get Acquainted

Chapter 2 emphasizes the concept of cultural diffusion. For example, the Egyptians adapted the bronze weapons of their conquerors, the Hyksos. In turn, Egyptian medical expertise was borrowed by other ancient civilizations.

TEACHER MATERIAL

Learning Objective To demonstrate the process of cultural diffusion.

Activity Groups of students representing different civilizations presented in the chapter will decide whether or not to adopt elements of the other cultures with which they interact.

Teacher Preparation Copy the form on the next page, one per student, and make an extra one for each group's final list.

Activity Guidelines

1. Introduce the activity by discussing the concept of cultural diffusion. Give an example such as how the people of Mesopotamia under Sargon's rule began to use the Akkadian language instead of Sumerian. Have students give examples of elements of other cultures they encounter every day. (*ethnic foods, music, technology, fashion*)

2. Explain to students that they will simulate, in a small and simple way, how cultural diffusion occurs.

3. Distribute the forms and organize the class into groups. Assign one of the ancient civilizations (Egyptian, Mesopotamian, Harappan, Chinese) to each group.

4. Have group members list on their forms any element of their assigned culture they can find in the text.

5. Group members then meet and choose a group leader. The group leader conducts a discussion of the assigned culture and records the group's list under "Elements of Our Civilization."

6. Next, have all groups exchange cultural information. From what it has determined about its own culture, each group decides which elements it can use from the other cultures. For example, the Harappan civilization may want to borrow the Sumerian writing system, whereas the Chinese may want to borrow Mesopotamia's laws and codes. Give groups a few minutes to finalize their lists of "Elements to Adopt from Other Cultures." Group leaders will record the groups' decisions.

7. When all groups have met, have each group leader present the original list and the list agreed upon after the interactions.

8. After all groups have presented, ask students to evaluate the exercise. Sample questions you may want to ask include:
   - How did you decide upon the elements you adopted from other cultures? (*Answers will vary, but students should consider the needs of the civilizations they represent.*)
   - What are some ways in which contacts among cultures may have occurred? (*through trade, war, exploration, migration*)
   - How are cultural elements diffused in today's world? (*Answers will vary, but students should mention that high-tech communications and high-speed transportation systems help diffuse cultural elements.*)
   - How is this demonstration different from the way in which cultural diffusion normally occurs? (*Students should understand that it occurs over a long period of time and there usually are no purposeful meetings to exchange information.*)

Name .... Date .... Class ....

History Simulation 2

HANDOUT MATERIAL

Let's Get Acquainted—Worksheet

CIVILIZATION: _____

	Elements of Our Civilization	Elements to Adopt from Other Cultures
Religion		
Government		
Technology		
Artistic Achievements		
Other		

History Simulation 3

Talking Heads

Innovation often results from the exchange of ideas. The Aramaeans and the Phoenicians spread their ideas and cultural innovations throughout the region through trade.

TEACHER MATERIAL

Learning Objective To illustrative the relationship between cultural diffusion and innovation.

Activity Time and space have collapsed and pairs of historical figures from the ancient Middle East are making the talk show circuit on American television. Even though they are from different cultures and lived at different times, these visitors have always wanted to talk to each other. Being interested in other cultures, they are also very eager to meet twentieth-century Americans. To do all these things, they need a production group that can help them organize their ideas, write their script, and present their conversation.

Teacher Preparation Bring in reference books for background information. Also have students construct a simple studio set. This might include a backdrop (world map, tapestry, etc.), cardboard tubing and plastic foam balls painted black for microphones, and chairs. Make one copy of the planning worksheet on the next page for each group.

Activity Guidelines

1. Explain to students that they are to prepare a talk show dialogue between two people from the ancient Middle East.

2. Organize the class into small groups. Give a copy of the handout to each group. Advise groups to plan their time carefully because they will be giving five-minute presentations to the whole class.

3. Instruct students to decide on the roles each member of their group will take. These might include:
   - Actors
   - Publicity person
   - Host
   - Director
   - Props Master
   - Audience members with questions

4. Have each group select a pair of historical figures from the list below:
   - Phoenician alphabet inventor and Ashurbanipal
   - Aramaean merchant and Persian road engineer
   - Moses and Zoroaster
   - Nebuchadnezzar and Solomon
   - Phoenician sailor and Chaldean stargazer

5. All members of a group should participate in researching and writing the scripts. Allow groups 15 minutes to prepare their presentations: 5 minutes for brainstorming and research and 10 minutes for actual scripting.

6. Have the groups assemble at the interview area and give their presentations. Allow about seven minutes per group for setup and presentation.

7. Close the activity by holding a class discussion. Ask the groups to respond to these questions about cultural diffusion and diversity, drawing on their experience producing the talk show dialogue.
   - Which cultural elements are most easily accepted by other cultures?
   - What benefits and what problems arise from cultural diversity?

Encourage students to give examples from the dialogue to support their ideas.

Name .... Date .... Class ....

HISTORY SIMULATION 3

HANDOUT MATERIAL

Talking Heads

Select one of these pairs for your talk show.

- ☐ Phoenician alphabet inventor and Ashurbanipal
- ☐ Aramaean merchant and Persian road engineer
- ☐ Phoenician sailor and Chaldean stargazer
- ☐ Moses and Zoroaster
- ☐ Nebuchadnezzar and Solomon

| Actors | Props Master | Audience members with questions | Other |

| Host | Director | Publicity |

Introduction by host (30 seconds): _____

_____

Ideas of topics to be discussed in talk (3–4 minutes): _____

_____

_____

Questions from host or audience (1 minute): _____

_____

_____

History Simulation 4

Visiting History

Events in the history of ancient Greece illustrate three major concepts: relation to the environment, movement, regionalism, and conflict. These events range from moments in the lives of ancient Minoans as depicted in frescoes excavated by archaeologists of the 1800s to battles in the Persian Wars as recorded by the historian Herodotus.

TEACHER MATERIAL

Learning Objective To illustrate the chapter concepts of relation to the environment, movement, regionalism, and conflict.

Activity Groups of students will prepare and present segments of a television special titled "Visiting History." Each segment will deal with a specific event from the chapter and illustrate one or more of the chapter concepts.

Teacher Preparation Make enough copies of the next page to provide one or two per group.

Activity Guidelines

1. Introduce the activity by reviewing the chapter concepts. Have students turn to page 104 in their textbooks and ask a volunteer to read the Chapter Themes.

2. Tell students that they will prepare a segment of a television documentary titled "Visiting History." Explain that the objective of the program is to act out events in history in order to bring the events to life for the audience and to illustrate the chapter concepts in relation to historical events.

3. Organize the class into four groups and assign each group one of these events: excavation of the palace at Knossos, establishment of Greek colonies, Battle of Salamis, Solon's rule.

4. Distribute the planning forms and direct students to divide among group members the tasks involved in preparing and presenting their program segments. Remind students that they will be evaluated on their cooperative participation. Tasks include completing the planning form, preparing research notes, writing the script from research notes, acting, and announcing.

5. Suggest that students use the following format for their presentations:

   - An anchor announces what the audience is about to witness, emphasizing the concept that will be stressed in the interview.

   - A reporter on the scene interviews celebrities (historical figures discussed in the chapter) or people on the street. For example, for the excavation at Knossos, reporters could interview Sir Arthur Evans and/or his assistants. The archaeologists explain what has been uncovered and how they interpret their findings; for example, the murals on the palace walls suggest lifestyles and occupations that, in turn, indicate the Minoans' relationship to their environment.

6. Assume the role of announcer to introduce the segments or have students choose someone to do so. After all presentations have been made, have the groups come together to evaluate each segment of the program by asking them:

   - How were the concept or concepts conveyed in this segment of the program?

   - What were some of the group's organizational problems? How did you resolve them?

   - Which criteria would you use to rate the overall group presentation?

Name .... Date .... Class ....

HISTORY SIMULATION 4

HANDOUT MATERIAL

Visiting History—Planning Form

Event (check one):
- ☐ Excavation of the Palace at Knossos
- ☐ Establishment of Greek Colonies
- ☐ Battle of Salamis
- ☐ Solon's Rule

Assignments:

Researchers	Scriptwriters	Actors	Other
_____	_____	_____	_____
_____	_____	_____	_____
_____	_____	_____	_____
_____	_____	_____	_____

Concepts to be illustrated:

_____
_____
_____
_____
_____
_____
_____

General plan for presentation:

_____
_____
_____
_____
_____
_____
_____
_____

HISTORY SIMULATION 5

Playing Aristotle

Aristotle influenced philosophers and scientists who lived after him. He originated a technique for investigating and analyzing data that is followed in the scientific method of today—first, collecting and observing facts; next, analyzing similarities and differences, advantages and disadvantages; and finally, developing conclusions and generalities.

TEACHER MATERIAL

Learning Objective To apply Aristotle's technique of analyzing information to topics in ancient history.

Activity Groups of students will model Aristotle's technique—gather facts, analyze the information, and reach conclusions about an assigned topic. Groups will then take turns presenting their conclusions to the class.

Teacher Preparation Make enough copies of the next page to give one worksheet to each student, plus four extra copies for the group presentations.

Activity Guidelines

1. Introduce the activity by asking students what is involved in Aristotle's technique of investigating and analyzing data before reaching a conclusion. Refer them to page 137 in the textbook. Then have a volunteer give an example of how Aristotle applied this technique. (*Aristotle's investigation and analysis before he wrote* Politics)

2. Tell students that they are going to apply Aristotle's technique to specific topics.

3. Organize the class into four groups A–D and distribute the worksheets. Group members should take on the tasks of researchers, recorder of discussion, leader of discussion, and presenters of the group's conclusions.

4. Student researchers use the "Facts" section of the worksheet to record their notes about their topic—Aristotle's observation step. (They should find information about each topic in the student text, but further research can be conducted.)

5. When research is completed, the researchers share their facts with the group. Give group members time to record and study the facts. Each group then discusses the facts and agrees on similarities and differences as one group member leads the discussion and another group member records the group's analysis of the facts—Aristotle's classification step.

6. The group then agrees on a conclusion or conclusions based on its investigation of the facts—Aristotle's generalization step. A student should record the group's conclusions.

7. The group decides on a method for one or two students to present the group's conclusions. Suggest that groups include some type of visual with their presentations. (*Conclusions will vary, but accept any that reflect an understanding of the topic. Possible conclusions: Group A—The two philosophers differed in their views of politics. If students conclude that one view or the other is better, they should defend their positions. Group B—Sophism might be more readily adopted by a person interested in entering politics. Group C—Alexander was more ambitious than Sargon I and gained more territory for his empire. Group D—Egypt may have had the better situation geographically; that is, both good farmland along the Nile and access to the sea.*)

8. Have students make their presentations, then ask them to evaluate the activity. Sample questions to ask students include:
   - How can you apply this technique to other subjects you study?
   - What did you find as the most difficult part of the process? Why?

World History   History Simulations   9

Name .... Date .... Class ....

History Simulation 5

HANDOUT MATERIAL

Playing Aristotle—Worksheet

Assignments
- ☐ **Group A**
  Investigate the political views of Plato and Aristotle.
- ☐ **Group B**
  Investigate Sophism and Stoicism.
- ☐ **Group C**
  Investigate the military and political accomplishments of Sargon I (Chapter 2) and Alexander the Great.
- ☐ **Group D**
  Investigate the civilizations of ancient Greece (Chapter 4) and Egypt (Chapter 2) relative to their geographic features.

Facts
_____
_____
_____
_____
_____

Similarities	Differences

Conclusions
_____
_____
_____
_____
_____

HISTORY SIMULATION 6

A Roman Mural

For each period of Roman history there are a few specific events or a few persons who truly represent the overall significance of that period.

TEACHER MATERIAL

Learning Objective To identify through art the main ideas and concepts of specific periods in Roman history.

Activity Small groups of students will plan, research, and prepare a wall mural of significant events and persons from a specific period of Roman history. Possible topics are: the legend of Romulus and Remus; the plebeians' struggle against the patricians; each of the three Punic Wars; the First Triumvirate; the Second Triumvirate; various aspects of life under the *Pax Romana*; the various invasions and the final decline and fall of Rome.

Teacher Preparation Make one copy of the next page for each group to use during the planning session. To complete the mural, each group will need a roll of paper at least 11 inches x 6 feet and colored markers or colored pencils. Have each group work on a long table, or clear space so that students can work on the floor.

Activity Guidelines

1. Remind students that much knowledge about Etruscan civilization comes from wall paintings in Etruscan tombs. Refer students to pages 105, 155, and 161 and ask them to compare how Etruscan wall paintings, the Standard of Ur, Minoan murals, as well as modern cartoon strips each tell a story. Introduce the activity to students by explaining its objective and general steps. Ask students to imagine that, as was the case with the Etruscan wall paintings, no written records have been deciphered about the events they are depicting, and their murals will be the only record historians of the future will have. Point out that historians can learn much about a culture from the clothing, jewelry, weaponry, and other artifacts depicted in wall paintings. Encourage students to be as accurate as possible about such details in their murals.

2. Organize students into groups of three to four. Assign an era, event, or series of events to each group. Distribute one copy of the planning guide on the next page to each group, instructing the groups to choose one member to fill out the guide.

3. To plan its mural, each group should determine the most important ideas about the topic assigned and write those ideas on the guide. Each group member should then choose one or more of the ideas to illustrate. The group should discuss how best to illustrate that idea and write a brief description of the illustration(s) in the space provided next to each group member's assignment. Each group member should keep personal notes about his or her assignment.

4. After the planning session and before the final session, students should individually prepare the designs and make sketches of their assigned illustrations. Encourage students to refer to illustrations in their textbooks and use library resources.

5. At the second session, distribute the mural paper and the markers or pencils so that groups can complete their murals.

6. After the murals are completed, have groups display them to the class and have students evaluate them. Sample questions you may want to ask include:
   - How well did each mural depict the main ideas of its topic?
   - What could historians of the future learn from each mural?

World History   History Simulations

Name .... Date .... Class ....

HISTORY SIMULATION 6

HANDOUT MATERIAL

Planning Guide for a Roman Mural

Topic _____

Important Ideas the Mural Should Convey:

1. _____
2. _____
3. _____
4. _____
5. _____
6. _____

Student Name	Ideas Assigned	Description of Illustrations

12   History Simulations   World History

HISTORY SIMULATION 7

Culture Quest

The ancient African Kingdoms of Kush, Axum, Mali, and the East African city-states grew and developed in concert with other cultures. Each civilization borrowed or modified a cultural element from a neighboring group of people, from those they traded with, or through conquest or travel. When a group of people borrows the language, the religion, or the customs of another culture, that group of people exhibit evidence of cultural diffusion.

TEACHER MATERIAL

Learning Objective To identify evidence of cultural diffusion among the early African kingdoms and within the students' own community.

Activity In groups of five or six, students will find evidence from their textbook or library resources of cultural diffusion in the ancient African kingdoms of Kush, Axum, Mali, and the East African city-states. Students will brainstorm evidence of cultural diffusion in their own community.

Teacher Preparation Bring to class the following items or close substitutes:

- reference books with illustrations demonstrating some of the cultural influences on the household objects, architecture, foods, or clothing of the early African civilizations. Examples: Kush—Roman, Assyrian, Egyptian influences; Axum—Egyptian, Greek, Roman, Persian, Indian influences; Mali—Arab world, Persian, Spanish influences; East Africa—Arab world, Indian, Persian, Chinese, Portuguese influences
- drawing paper
- 1 copy of the chart on page 14 for each group

Activity Guidelines

1. Organize the class into small groups. Explain that they will find evidence from their textbooks and library resources of cultural diffusion occurring in early African kingdoms. They should also brainstorm ideas about how their own community reflects cultural diffusion. Explain that groups will be evaluated on organization, cooperation, and factual accuracy.

2. Have each group select a manager, an artist, and a recorder.

3. Give each group recorder a copy of the chart on page 14.

4. Instruct students to work together to find each cultural group in the textbook and identify all the outside influences that affected that culture. Remind students of the means of cultural diffusion—contact with other peoples through migrations, trade, invasions, or geographical necessities. Then have students brainstorm ideas about how their own community demonstrates cultural diffusion from several cultures.

5. The recorder writes the information on the chart and cites the references.

6. The artist draws a sketch to represent the cultural element that was adopted by the civilization. Example: Kush—Egyptian pyramids.

7. Bring all the groups together to compare their answers. Have them evaluate themselves on cooperation, organization, and factual accuracy. Then discuss the cultural elements they found that exist in their own community.

Name .... Date .... Class ....

History Simulation 7

Culture Quest—Evidence Chart

HANDOUT MATERIAL

Use your textbook and classroom resources to find evidence of cultural diffusion among the early African kingdoms listed on the chart.

CULTURAL DIFFUSION CHART

Civilization	Outside Influences	Text Pages
Kush		
Axum		
Mali		
East Africa		
Your Community		

14 History Simulations World History

History Simulation 8

Cast in Stone

The invading Aryans introduced a system of four classes known as *varnas*, later called castes, to India's social structure. The following activity explores the specific duties associated with each *varna*.

TEACHER MATERIAL

Learning Objective To deepen an understanding of the Indian caste system and the importance of duty as revealed in Vedic writings.

Activity Students work in small groups to compose original "legends" that illustrate particular duties associated with the four *varnas* in the Aryan social system. Each group will be randomly assigned a caste. The group will then examine the duties of the caste, select one duty, and write a legend about it. Groups may also choose to make drawings to accompany their legends.

Teacher Preparation Each group will need writing paper or lined chart paper, pencils or markers, and drawing paper. Each student will need a copy of the handout material on page 16.

Activity Guidelines

1. Introduce the activity by explaining its objective and general steps. Briefly review the story of Arjuna on page 200 of Chapter 8. Discuss the duty illustrated in the story and how the duty relates to Arjuna's caste. Point out the dialogue between Arjuna and the Hindu god Krishna.

2. Organize students into four groups and assign each group a caste—Brahmans, Kshatriyas, Vaisyas, and Sudras. Assign each group an area in the classroom. Give groups the necessary materials. Call attention to the chart on the handout, and instruct the members of each group to use it as they:

- review the duties of their assigned caste as described in the text (students may also research to supplement their knowledge of the social classes and respective duties)
- select a duty to illustrate in a legend
- brainstorm to create characters and a basic story line for the legend (encourage students to review their knowledge of the Hindu gods or to research to learn more; point out that students should try to include several events and characters, developing a legend that is more involved than the brief incident about Arjuna; encourage students to include dialogue and try to achieve the essence of Vedic writings)
- write the legend as a group, with one student recording the story on writing paper or on chart paper as it is developed
- make drawings that show key events in the story
- review the legend, discussing the questions at the bottom of the chart.

3. After groups have finished writing their legends, have a class reading and discussion. Have one student from each group read the the group's legend. As each legend is read, discuss as a class the questions on the chart.

Name .... Date .... Class ....

HISTORY SIMULATION 8

HANDOUT MATERIAL

Cast in Stone

Group	☐ Brahmans	☐ Kshatriyas	☐ Vaisyas	☐ Sudras

Caste _____

Duties _____
_____
_____
_____
_____
_____
_____

Duty to be illustrated in legend: _____

List and briefly describe the characters you will include.

Characters	Description
_____	_____
_____	_____
_____	_____
_____	_____

Story line: Jot down the key events you will include.
_____
_____
_____
_____

Briefly discuss the following questions in your group.
- Is the duty illustrated in the legend appropriate to the caste?
- Does the legend show the importance of doing one's duty?
- Does the legend have the flavor of Vedic writings?

HISTORY SIMULATION 9

China Challenge

Chinese civilization made significant political, philosophical, cultural, and scientific advances during the Zhou, Qin, and Han dynasties. Innovations made during this period influenced Chinese family life, government, and art for centuries.

TEACHER MATERIAL

Learning Objective To review the great dynasties, three ways of life, and society and culture of ancient China.

Activity In groups of five or six, students will prepare for and compete in a game of China Challenge, based on the material found in Chapter 9. Each group will develop a list of four categories, then develop four questions for each category. Groups will then exchange question sets. Using the sets of questions obtained from another group, members of each group will then compete in China Challenge.

Teacher Preparation Each group will need a supply of index cards; a clock or watch with a second hand. Provide each group with one copy of the scorecard on the next page. Make sure students have their textbooks available.

Activity Guidelines

1. Introduce the activity to the students by summarizing the period of Chinese history covered in Chapter 9. Explain the objective of China Challenge.

2. Organize students into groups of five or six and distribute the materials. Have each group choose a group leader and a scorekeeper.

3. Have each group brainstorm a list of four categories for questions. Some possibilities are: Inventions, Religions, Potpourri, People, Words That Begin with S (for example, Sima Qian, *Spring and Autumn Annals*, Silk Road). The group leader should record each category on a separate index card.

4. The group leader should assign two categories to subgroups of two or three. Subgroups then use their textbooks to develop a set of four questions for each of the categories assigned to them. Questions should progress in difficulty and be assigned point values from 1 to 4, with 4 the most difficult. Each category should have one question at each level of difficulty. Have students write the category for each question at the upper left-hand corner of an index card, the point value at the upper right-hand corner, the question on the front, and the answer on the back. When all questions are complete, the group leader should collect all the cards and collate them in ascending level of difficulty under the index card on which the category title is written. Each group then exchanges its set of questions for those from another group.

5. After the scorekeeper fills out the scorecard the game begins. The first student chooses the category and level of difficulty of the question that he or she wants to answer. The scorekeeper then reads that question and allows 15 seconds for the student to answer. The scorekeeper then records the student's score. Questions unanswered or answered incorrectly are put in a separate pile to be used after all other questions are answered. Play continues until all questions are answered.

6. Have groups total their scores and announce winners. Collect all the sets of questions so that students can evaluate them. Sample questions you may want to ask include:
   - Why did you choose the categories you did?
   - Did the game help you master the material?

Name .... Date .... Class ....

HISTORY SIMULATION 9

HANDOUT MATERIAL

China Challenge—Scorecard

Scorekeeper: Use the chart below to record the scores of each group member playing China Challenge. In the four boxes across the top, write each of the categories. In the boxes along the left side, write the name of the group members. As a group member answers a question correctly, write the number of points he or she has earned under the appropriate category. At the end of the game, total the number of points for each student under each category, then write the grand total of all the points for each student in the column at the far right.

Categories

Student Name ▼					Grand Total ▼

18 History Simulations World History

History Simulation 10

Illumination

Chapter 10 discusses how the Byzantine Empire's geographic location, close ties to the Christian religion, and varied cultural achievements affected the course of its 1,000–year history. This activity calls for students to work together to understand certain elements of Byzantine society.

TEACHER MATERIAL

Learning Objective To "illuminate" some facts about Byzantine and Slavic civilizations.

Activity Two teams will develop and play a game based on information from this chapter, including the special features and photograph and art captions. Students will first meet as teams, then divide into smaller working groups of two to four within each team to develop questions and answers for five categories: geography, religion, art, people, and history. After recording the questions and answers on color-coded cards, each team will turn the cards in to you. You can then begin the game.

Teacher Preparation Make a copy of the Illumination worksheet for each student. Gather the following supplies: 60 index cards, 5 different-colored marking pens, 5 white letter-sized envelopes, and a one-minute timer.

Activity Guidelines

1. Explain to students that they are to develop a game based on material from this chapter to help them learn and recall key facts about the Byzantines and Slavs.

2. Organize the class into two teams. Then subdivide each team into five groups of two to four, depending on the number of students per team. Give each team 30 index cards and a worksheet for each student.

3. Explain that students are to work together to develop six questions and answers in each of the five categories. (List the categories on the chalkboard.) Each group within a team will choose one of the categories. Have each student write questions and answers on paper, then let each group choose six to record on index cards, putting the question on one side and the answer on the other.

4. Allow half of one class period for game preparation. Have teams turn in the five sets of cards to you when they are completed. Put all cards of one category into an envelope and mark the outside with one of the colored pens to designate the category.

5. Allow another whole or half period to play the game. One team selects a category. The other team reads the ANSWER from a card, sets the one-minute timer, and tries to come up with a question to fit it. Team members may confer. Play passes to the other team if the response is incorrect. Each correct response counts 5 points. Continue until all cards have been used. The team with the highest score wins.

Name .... Date .... Class ....

History Simulation 10

HANDOUT MATERIAL

Illumination—Worksheet

Check the box next to your group's category:

☐ Geography   ☐ Religion   ☐ Art   ☐ People   ☐ History

Question/Answer Sheet

1. Q _____
   A _____
2. Q _____
   A _____
3. Q _____
   A _____
4. Q _____
   A _____
5. Q _____
   A _____
6. Q _____
   A _____

Team Score: _____

HISTORY SIMULATION 11

Understanding Islam

This activity is designed to provide students with the opportunity to work together to understand various aspects of Islamic history.

TEACHER MATERIAL

Learning Objective To reinforce students' understanding of people, places, events, and causes and effects related to Islam.

Activity Students will form six groups to prepare and answer questions in the categories stated above. Two teams at a time will compete in answering each other's questions. The two highest-scoring teams then compete to determine the final winner.

Teacher Preparation Collect timing devices. Provide enough index cards for the entire class. Make enough copies of the handout for one or two members per team.

Activity Guidelines

1. Introduce the activity. Explain that each team member will review the chapter and prepare one question and answer on one side of an index card for each of four categories: People, Places, Events, and Causes and Effects. (You may want to give an example of the last category: How did the geography of the Arabian Peninsula affect the bedouin who lived there?) Have each team write two extra questions to avoid possible duplications.

2. Organize the class into six teams and have each team choose a captain. Students write their questions and answers, which are then assigned point values of 5, 10, 15, 20, or 25 to indicate the level of difficulty. The point value is written on each card. The team members submit their questions for review to their captain, who then separates the cards by category and replaces any duplications.

3. Assign two members of each team to serve as scorekeeper and timekeeper. Then designate three sets of two teams to compete.

4. Teams take turns asking and answering questions. Each member of the "answer" team selects a category and the point value of the question to be answered, such as People for 5 points. The opposing team captain then asks the appropriate question from the index cards. Allow 15 seconds for the answer. The team that begins continues as long as it answers correctly. Then teams switch roles.

5. The scorekeeper checks the appropriate column on the scorecard for both category and point value.

6. The team that has the highest total after 25 minutes wins. The two highest-scoring teams then meet to determine the final winner of the competition.

World History

Name .... Date .... Class ....

HISTORY SIMULATION 11

HANDOUT MATERIAL

Understanding Islam

Scorecard

Point Value	People	Places	Events	Causes and Effects
5				
10				
15				
20				
25				

Subtotals: _____ _____ _____ _____

Total: _____

HISTORY SIMULATION 12

Meet the Medievals

This activity reflects the nature of life in medieval western Europe—how strong leadership, security, loyalty, cooperation, and hard work were all necessary for survival.

TEACHER MATERIAL

Learning Objective To introduce students to the people of the Middle Ages, their social standings, and the economic, political, and spiritual interdependency that characterized medieval life.

Activity This activity should be done before students begin reading Chapter 12. Six students will read aloud from the character descriptions on the worksheet on page 24. The first student will introduce Lord Godwin to the class; the second student will introduce Lady Elizabeth, and so on, until all six characters have been introduced. Then lead a discussion using the questions on the worksheet in order to enhance students' understanding of medieval society and to prepare them for information presented in the chapter.

Teacher Preparation Make one copy of the handout material for each student.

Activity Guidelines

1. Introduce the activity by discussing the concept of interdependence in general. For example, students are dependent on their families, teachers, and friends for certain necessities, such as food and shelter, learning and guidance, or emotional support. People also depend on the students: friends need emotional support from them; employers count on them to do a good job; and parents expect them to work hard in school and abide by rules. Tell students that medieval society was in many ways similar to their own situation.

2. Explain to students that during this activity they will meet six people of the Middle Ages who come from different social levels and have different needs and responsibilities. Mention that all these people, in one way or another, depended on other people in the social hierarchy.

3. Organize the class into six groups and ask for one volunteer from each group to read an introduction. Write the names *King Jeffrey* and *Lord Godwin* on the chalkboard to begin the diagram that will summarize the interdependent society. As each student introduces a new person, add that person to the diagram with arrows representing his or her connection to those already listed.

4. After all the characters are introduced, have the class discuss the questions in their groups. They must agree on the answers and present a group answer sheet. Each group should select a leader and a recorder and be prepared to discuss their answers with the other groups.

World History — History Simulations — 23

Name _____ Date _____ Class _____

History Simulation 12

HANDOUT MATERIAL

Meet the Medievals

Lord Godwin of Amsbury
I am Lord Godwin, in the service of King Jeffrey, now the ruler of this region of England. I am the owner of a large estate, granted me by the king in turn for my loyalty and my legions of knights. I am sworn to protect my king—a duty I hold as dear as my own life. But I am ambitious and have sent my knights to battle John of Lamprey, lord to King Richard, a possible usurper of the Crown.

Lady Elizabeth
I am wife to Lord Godwin and the mother of his seven children (two of which have died of the plague). I am mistress of the estate, which is no small task, for there are 100 servants, cooks, artisans, and peasants who need my attention. I also keep an herb garden for the medicines my household might need.

Sir Stephen
I am the son of Lord Godwin and will soon become a knight. I have spent several years as a page and squire to a neighboring lord, whom my father trusts. If I can prove myself at tourney, I will earn the right to bear arms for King Jeffrey. Someday he may grant me a fief for my bravery.

Mary, prioress of Saint Agatha
I am the daughter of Lord and Lady Godwin. I would not marry the man my father ordered me to marry, so I have taken refuge in the Convent of Saint Agatha. I will serve God and the good peasants of the nearby village with my skills in medicine that I learned from my mother.

Jack Builder
I am called Jack Builder because I am a mason, a skilled artisan. I have served many an important lord and clergyman. I was an apprentice to the master builder of King Jeffrey's castle, and I was master builder of the cathedral that serves Holy Cross in the Woods. The cathedral is the most important building in town.

Agnes
I am a serf who lives on the estate of Lord Godwin. I work on the estate with my husband and our three children. I pull a plow and sow seeds. In deep winter, I am invited to the great house to help with the needlework and mending. Godwin will always be my lord, unless Richard seizes the throne from King Jeffrey. Then this estate will be granted to John of Lamprey, and he will be our new lord.

1. Which people seem to have the most power? _____

   Which seem to have the least power? _____

2. Assumptions we can make about the quality of these people's lives:
   _____

3. The political situation here is subject to change. How is this related to the interdependency of various groups of people?
   _____
   _____

4. At this point, the character we would like to be is _____ because
   _____

History Simulation 13

The Duties of the Pope

This activity focuses on the significance of the Roman Catholic Church during the Middle Ages and the role that popes played in the social, economic, and political lives of medieval people.

TEACHER MATERIAL

Learning Objective To develop an understanding of the power, responsibilities, and problems of popes in the Middle Ages.

Activity Organize the class into five groups to represent the interests of European monarchs, peasants, the clergy, nobles, or Christians in Jerusalem. Group members will work together to decide how they would like the pope to act to best represent their interests. They will reach a consensus as a group and present their results to the class.

Teacher Preparation Copy the handout materials on the next page, making one copy for each group. Make sure students have their textbooks.

Activity Guidelines

1. Introduce the activity to students by explaining its objective. Then briefly review material in Chapter 13 related to popes. Remind students of the roles Pope Urban II, Pope Eugenius IV, and Pope Innocent III played in the Crusades. Review the abuses by the clergy and the challenge to church authority that occurred during the late Middle Ages.

2. Have students form groups representing the interests of segments of medieval society. They will have half a class period to develop their positions. In the last half of the period they will present and discuss results.

3. Distribute the handouts. Then have each group choose one member to read aloud the issues on the handout to the group and another member to record the group's decisions.

4. Group members should discuss their position on each issue, come to an agreement, and record their position and reasons for each of the seven issues on the handout.

5. Group members will take turns presenting their group's position on each issue to the class. For example, one monarch will present his or her group's position on the Crusades. Then a peasant will present his or her group's position on the same issue, and so on until all the groups have discussed the issue. Then different members of each group will discuss indulgences, and so on until all seven issues have been presented.

6. After the presentations, have the class consider how much political power each of the five groups had in medieval society. As a class, come to a consensus on whose positions would most likely have been adopted by the pope.

Name .... Date .... Class ....

HISTORY SIMULATION 13

HANDOUT MATERIAL

The Duties of the Pope—Position Chart

Issue	Group's Position	Reason(s)
1. Should the pope call for crusades to retake the Holy Lands?		
2. What should the pope do about selling indulgences and selling positions in the Church?		
3. Should the pope intervene in the affairs of towns—require taxes, services to lords, and obedience to feudal laws? Or should towns be self-governing?		
4. What should the pope do about the teachings of John Wycliffe and Jan Hus?		
5. Should the pope intervene to settle the Hundred Years' War?		
6. Should the pope intervene in education? Should he support the teachings of Aristotle?		
7. How much say should the pope have in the kind of literature or art that is produced?		

History Simulation 14

Territorial Tracks

Geography played an important role in the development of the early civilizations of East and South Asia. The people of Southeast Asia relied on the rivers that flow through their countries to grow and transport crops. China, Korea, and Japan benefited from the geographic barriers of mountains and seas that isolated their societies from external invasion and intervention.

TEACHER MATERIAL

Learning Objective To learn about the physical geography of China, Southeast Asia, Korea, and Japan.

Activity Three teams develop game materials using maps, atlases, and information from this chapter. Assign a specific country to each team. Team members write clues and answers about the landforms, waterways, climate, and cities of their assigned country; then play a geography game.

Teacher Preparation Make a copy of the handout material for each team. Gather the following supplies: a large wall map of East and South Asia, three atlases, pushpins with red, green, and yellow plastic heads, scissors for each team, and a container for the clues (shoe box or paper bag).

Activity Guidelines

1. Explain to students that they are going to develop clues for a game based on geographic facts about the Asian countries they studied in Chapter 14.

2. Organize the class into three teams and assign China to one team, Southeast Asia to another, and Korea and Japan to the third team. Give each team a copy of the handout material, scissors, an atlas, and a set of red, green, or yellow pushpins.

3. Explain that team members will work together to write clues and answers that describe landforms, waterways, climate, and cities of their assigned country.

4. Ask each team to choose a recorder. Then have the team develop 10 clues with answers about a city, waterway, or landform of their region. The recorder writes the clues on the clue sheet. Then each member cuts out one or two clue cards, folds them, and places them in the single container provided for all clues.

5. Allow approximately half of the class period for teams to make the clue cards. When all groups have placed their cards in the container, begin the game.

6. One student from one team chooses a clue from the container, reads the clue, and allows anyone from any of the other teams to respond. The team that makes the first correct answer sends its representative to the wall map and marks the spot of the answer with a team pin. The person who answered correctly reads the next clue. The game continues in this manner until all clues have been read. The team with the most pins on the map wins.

7. Encourage team members to discuss clues before giving their answers.

Name .... Date .... Class ....

History Simulation 14

HANDOUT MATERIAL

Territorial Tracks—Clue Sheet

| **Sample Clue:** A city located on a harbor and facing the Yellow Sea. | **Answer:** Seoul, Korea |

Clue: _____   Answer: _____

Clue: _____   Answer: _____

Clue: _____   Answer: _____

Clue: _____   Answer: _____

Clue: _____   Answer: _____

Clue: _____   Answer: _____

Clue: _____   Answer: _____

Clue: _____   Answer: _____

Clue: _____   Answer: _____

Clue: _____   Answer: _____

History Simulations — World History

History Simulation 15

Asking Around

Chapter 15 describes several great civilizations and empires of Mesoamerica and South America. Some of these empires lasted hundreds of years. Others were destroyed—prematurely, some might say—with the arrival of European explorers and conquerors.

TEACHER MATERIAL

Learning Objective To practice conducting interviews and recording information about a culture or civilization for purposes of preservation.

Activity In small groups, students will research and record information about a Mesoamerican or South American civilization. Possible topics include government, religion, calendars, foods, art, communications and trade, or rituals and sports.

Teacher Preparation Make one copy of the next page for each student. Bring in supplemental reference books and magazine articles for background information on the Maya, the Aztec, and the Inca civilizations. If students are to create their volumes in class (see guideline 4), have necessary art supplies such as paper and colored pencils or markers on hand. If students will be using school computers, arrange computer access if necessary.

Activity Guidelines

1. Tell students that much of what we know about the Aztec prior to the Spanish conquest comes from the work of a Franciscan priest, Fray Bernardino de Sahagún, who arrived in the Americas in 1529. He learned Nahuatl, the Aztec language, and recognizing that the Aztec culture was disappearing, spent decades creating a 12–volume description of every aspect of Aztec culture. His *General History of the Things of New Spain* is based on interviews with the last of the Aztec who remembered what life was like before the arrival of the Spanish.

2. Organize students into groups of four or six. Assign a civilization (Maya, Aztec, or Inca) and a topic to each group (see above). Ask students to decide which members of their group will be interviewers and which will be interviewees speaking as members of the civilization being studied. Distribute a copy of the worksheet to all the interviewers and have students fill in the name of the civilization and the topic.

3. The interviewees in each group will find information about the topic for their civilization, using the reference sources provided. They also will provide a picture—either from a reference source or one they have drawn themselves—of a scene or object that represents an important aspect of their topic. The interviewer will then ask appropriate questions and record the answers on the worksheet.

4. When the interviews are completed, the group will meet to plan a volume of information on the topic they have researched. Using either art supplies or computers, students can create a book that presents and preserves what they have learned.

Name _____ Date _____ Class _____

History Simulation 15

HANDOUT MATERIAL

Asking Around—Worksheet

Civilization _____

Topic _____

Interviewee _____   Interviewer _____

Ask questions such as the following as you conduct your interview:

What is this called?	Is it used by one person or many?
Where is it found?	How is it used?
Is it hard to find? Are there many of them?	What does it sound like/smell like/taste like/feel like?
Who uses it?	

Interviewer's Description or Sketch of Object:

Interviewer's Description or Sketch of Object:

Interviewer's Description or Sketch of Object:

Interviewer's Description or Sketch of Object:

Notes on Interview:

_____

_____

_____

_____

History Simulation 16

A Renaissance Fair

Sections 1 and 2 described the Italian Renaissance and its spread to northern Europe. As Europeans accepted ideas of humanism and secularism, many cities and towns supported the works of artists, writers, and philosophers.

TEACHER MATERIAL

Learning Objective To broaden students' knowledge and deepen their appreciation of the contributions of Renaissance culture.

Activity Groups of students work together to prepare fair booths (tables) representing selected aspects of Renaissance culture. Each group chooses a cultural focus, researches information about that Renaissance topic, and prepares an exhibit or demonstration such as posters, poetry, play readings, or models. On a designated day, all the groups present their displays or demonstrations. Group members take turns hosting their booths and answering questions about their chosen Renaissance topics. Students create and distribute surveys to visitors.

Teacher Preparation Provide for each group: poster board, colored markers, paper, tape, ruler. Make a copy of the handout on page 32 for each student. On the day of the fair, make available a folding table or a few desks for each group and clear a large area of the classroom, or schedule the use of another room for the fair.

Activity Guidelines

1. Introduce the activity to students by explaining its objective and general steps.

2. Organize students into groups of three or four and give a copy of the handout to each student.

3. Direct each group to choose one cultural aspect of the Renaissance using the list of subjects provided. Tell students that they may narrow their subject by focusing on one city or country. For example: architecture in Rome, literature in England, or painting in northern Europe.

4. Have each group write its subject on the board. Point out that two groups may choose the same subject if they change the focus, such as Italian painting and Dutch painting.

5. Set a date for the fair. Advertise it throughout the school.

6. Direct students to research their topics, consulting with art, literature, or music teachers and librarians as needed. Have groups plan and prepare posters for their booths. Depending on the subject, a booth might also include pictures of paintings, sculptures, or buildings. Encourage groups to cooperate in sharing resources, making copies from books if necessary. If groups are staging demonstrations or readings from literature, advise them to schedule rehearsals.

7. Before the day of the fair, direct groups to make schedules for hosting their booths so that all students will have time to view the various displays and demonstrations. As a class, design and create a survey form that can be handed out to visitors during the fair. The survey should include questions asking visitors what they have learned about the Renaissance and elicit further comments about the booths.

8. After the fair, have students review and discuss visitors' responses.

Name .... Date .... Class ....

History Simulation 16

HANDOUT MATERIAL

A Renaissance Fair

Steps for Staging a Renaissance Fair
1. Choose a subject from the list.
2. Choose a city or country on which to focus.
3. Plan and conduct research.
4. Share research findings with your group members.
5. Plan a poster and pictures, readings, or demonstrations for the fair booth.
6. Prepare the poster. Plan the layout of the booth pictures or rehearse readings or demonstrations.
7. Make a schedule showing the time for each group member to host the booth. Host should be prepared to answer questions.

Subjects for Renaissance Fair Booths
- ☐ Painting
- ☐ Architecture
- ☐ Sculpture
- ☐ Literature
- ☐ Music
- ☐ Sports and Games

Focus Country
- ☐ Germany and Low Countries
- ☐ Florence
- ☐ Rome
- ☐ Venice
- ☐ Italy
- ☐ France
- ☐ England

Items for Fair Booths
- Poster identifying subject and providing key information
- Pictures of paintings, sculptures, or buildings
- Readings from literature
- Musical recordings
- Demonstrations of sports or games

HISTORY SIMULATION 17

The Search for Andronia

During the age of exploration, European explorers used unsophisticated instruments to navigate their small sailing ships, searching for a water route to Asia. They faced the dangers of long voyages at sea—storms, lack of fresh food, disease, accidents, and the emotional stress of being away from home and family.

TEACHER MATERIAL

Learning Objective To understand the difficulties and risks explorers faced in charting unknown territories.

Activity Groups role-play a voyage of exploration searching for the fabled wealthy planet of Andronia. Voyagers draw one card at a time from a stack of game cards, each of which describes a part of the journey. The group then decides how to respond to that event; points are awarded according to their responses. When all groups have completed their journeys, they compare their point totals.

Teacher Preparation Cut the game cards apart, keeping them in sets. Each group needs one copy of the handout, paper and pencil for keeping score, and a coin to flip.

Activity Guidelines

1. Explain the objective and general directions.
2. To help students prepare for the game, set the following scene:
   Andronia is a planet of fabulous wealth. It contains enormous deposits of gold and silver, huge veins of which can clearly be seen in the bare sides of cliffs. However, no ship has ever returned from a journey to Andronia. What is known of the planet comes secondhand from traders from other planets in the galaxy. It is uncertain whether the planet's location is shown accurately on existing star maps. Furthermore, there are many dangers: black holes that swallow ships whole; electromagnetic fields that burn a ship's electronic system, leaving it adrift in space; and reaching the edge of the known universe and slipping into the Great Void, from which there is no return.
3. Organize the class into small groups and have each group choose a captain. Give each group 1,000 points. Tell them that the captain has absolute authority. In the case of mutiny, the group will elect a new captain.
4. Distribute one set of game cards, turned face-down, to each group.
5. Groups begin the game by choosing a card and reading it aloud. They then discuss the situation and decide the response—go on, turn back, or take some other course of action. The captain makes the final decision, either by consulting the group or making the decision unilaterally. The group has the option of mutiny at any time. The game continues until the crew turns back, stays in one location, or uses all game cards.
6. When all groups have completed the game, have all groups that did not turn back or settle on another planet choose outcome letter *a*, *b*, or *c*. Then read the outcome each group selected from the list below. Groups count their points. The group with the most points wins.
   a. Andronia is even richer than legend has told. All crew members become fabulously wealthy and return home to live happily ever after. Add 50,000 points.
   b. Andronia contains no riches. It does, however, have enough food and water to sustain life and reprovision the ship for the journey home. Deduct 20,000 points.
   c. The crew realizes too late that the ship has been pulled off course by electromagnetic forces. It sails into oblivion. Deduct all points.
7. Have groups compare the difficulties each group faced to the hardships of European explorers in the 1500s.

World History · History Simulations · 33

History Simulation 17

HANDOUT MATERIAL

The Search for Andronia

The Search for Andronia — Game Card 1

You have been traveling for more than two months and should have reached Andronia long ago. You may be nearing the edge of the Great Void.

Turn Back
Your voyage is over. 500 points

Or—flip a coin:
HEADS, you recheck your map and figure out where you are. 15,000 points
TAILS, you wander for five years before returning to familiar territory. 2,000 points

---

The Search for Andronia — Game Card 2

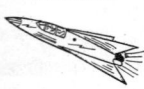

You have drifted into fierce solar winds from a nearby star. If you continue, your ship may break apart.

Turn Back
Your voyage is over. 500 points

Or—flip a coin:
HEADS, you survive. 2,000 points
TAILS, your ship is damaged. −2,000 points

The Search for Andronia — Game Card 3

The fuel regenerator has broken and might not be repairable. You have fuel for two weeks, after which your ship will drift aimlessly in space. If you turn back now, you will reach home before fuel runs out.

Turn Back
Your voyage is over. 500 points

Or—flip a coin:
HEADS, you fix the regenerator. 3,000 points
TAILS, it can't be fixed. Sail on and cross your fingers. −3,000 points

---

The Search for Andronia — Game Card 4

You are approaching an asteroid belt. If you attempt to navigate through it, your ship will almost surely be crushed.

Turn Back
Your voyage is over. 500 points

Or—flip a coin:
HEADS, you survive. 3,000 points
TAILS, your ship is damaged. −3,000 points

The Search for Andronia — Game Card 5

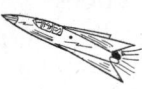

You have encountered an uncharted planet much like Earth, with many resources. The inhabitants are friendly and invite you to stay. You may be able to set up a trading station on the planet.

Stay
Your voyage is over. 5,000 points

Continue
15,000 points

The Search for Andronia — Game Card 6

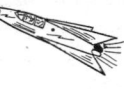

Food is running very low. Each crew member is rationed to two slices of bread each day. Some crew members are becoming ill from a lack of vitamins in their diet.

Turn Back
Your voyage is over. 500 points

Or—flip a coin:
HEADS, no one becomes seriously ill. 3,000 points
TAILS, some crew members are incapacitated. −3,000 points

---

34 History Simulations World History

History Simulation 18

Empire Bingo

From A.D. 1400 to 1700, Asian empires arose in Central Asia, India, China, and Japan to become powerful political forces within their regions. At the same time, these empires experienced great cultural advances.

TEACHER MATERIAL

Learning Objective To become familiar with basic facts about Asian empires.

Activity Three groups prepare questions with one-word answers for a game based on information from Chapter 18. Groups compete in a class game of Empire Bingo.

Teacher Preparation Make one copy of the game card for each student. Have on hand the following supplies: three sheets of paper for the questions and answers and paper clips for students to use as game markers.

Activity Guidelines

1. Explain to students that they are to develop 24 questions and answers for a game called Empire Bingo based on facts from Chapter 18.

2. Organize the class into four groups to develop the question-and-answer sheets. Assign one section of Chapter 18 to each group. Give each group a sheet of paper and ask the groups to designate a recorder.

3. Explain that each group must work together to brainstorm six questions that require one-word answers. Sample question: Which early Ottoman emperor was known as "the Codifier" for his work in organizing Ottoman laws? (*Suleiman I*) The recorder writes the questions and answers on the paper. Allow about 10 minutes for this part of the activity. Then collect the question-and-answer sheets.

4. Next, give each group a game card. As you call out the one-word answers, students should write them on any space of the game card. There will be one free space on each card, and it can be anywhere. Allow another 10 minutes for this part of the activity. When this is completed, supply each player with some paper clips and Bingo can begin.

5. Ask one student to serve as quizmaster. The person who will serve as quizmaster reads each question, and players place a clip on the proper answer on the card. Remind students that the free space on the card automatically gets a clip. When a group has covered answers on five spaces that spell BINGO (the answers don't have to be all in the same row), they call out BINGO! In their group, students should repeat the question for each of their answers. The winning team earns 1 point.

6. A student from the winning team becomes the next quizmaster. He or she mixes up the questions and begins a new game. At the end of the class period, the team with the most points wins.

Name .... Date .... Class ....

History Simulation 18

HANDOUT MATERIAL

Empire

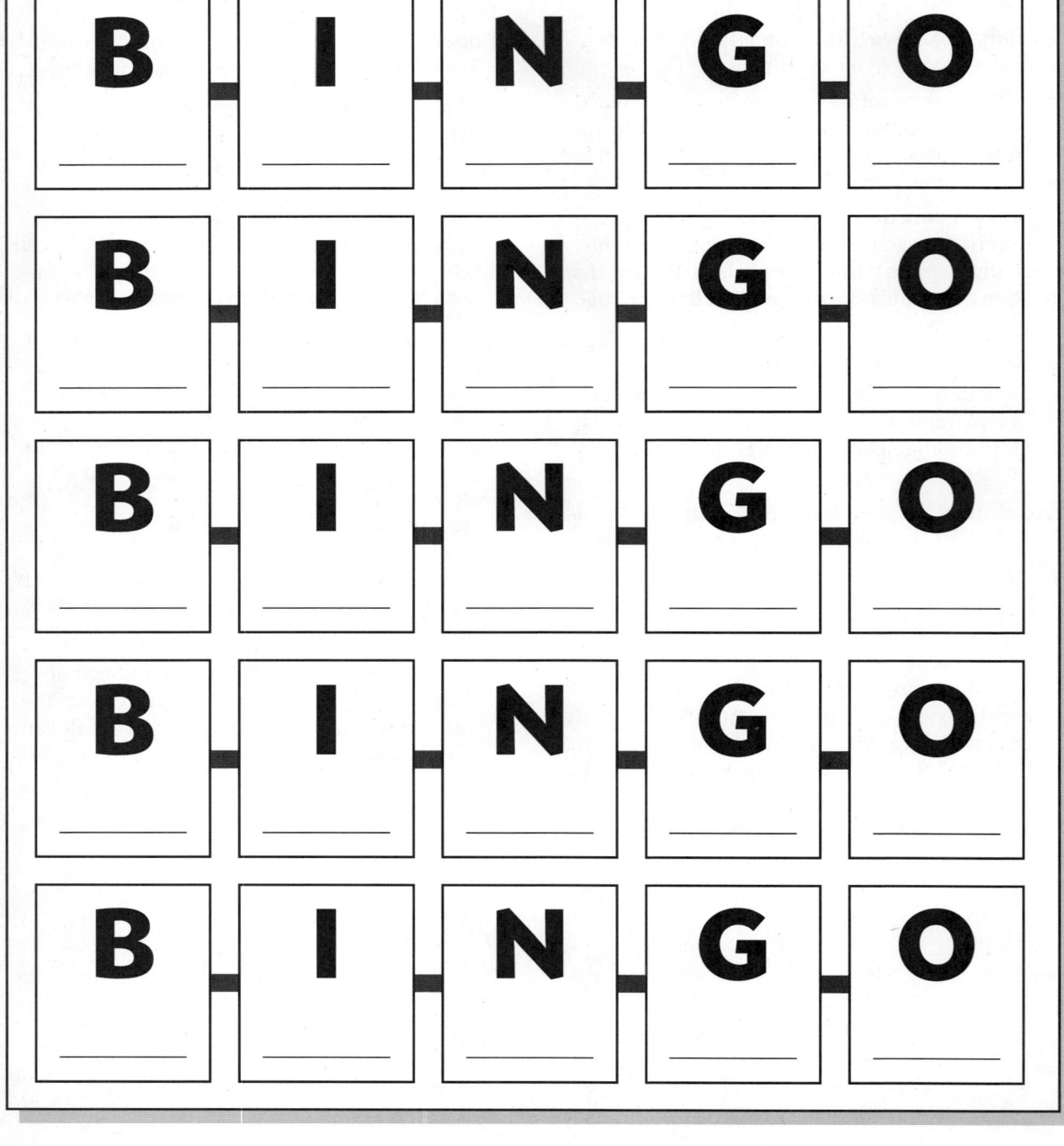

B	I	N	G	O
B	I	N	G	O
B	I	N	G	O
B	I	N	G	O
B	I	N	G	O

History Simulation 19

King or Queen for a Day

The age of absolute monarchs brought many social and political changes to the people and the map of Europe from 1500 to 1700. Kings and queens of Europe and Russia wielded absolute power over their subjects. Sometimes their rule brought benefits to the societies they ruled, but often this was at the expense of hardships to some groups.

TEACHER MATERIAL

Learning Objective To review and evaluate the political policies, military strategies, moral convictions, and personal objectives of the absolute monarchs who ruled from 1500 to 1700.

Activity Students will work in five groups to investigate and select the monarch they feel was the most influential to his or her time period and country. Groups should take into consideration how the monarch treated the common people and affected religious beliefs.

Teacher Preparation Each member of the group will need a copy of the worksheet on page 38 and a pencil or pen.

Activity Guidelines

1. Introduce this as a chapter-concluding activity that will require students to use all the knowledge they have gathered on the rulers and the countries involved. Explain the learning objective. Briefly review the major figures from each section.

2. Organize the class into five groups—one for each section of the text—and distribute copies of the worksheet. Explain that each group's task is to work together to come to a consensus about which monarch they would select to give the King- or Queen-for-a-Day-award to. The groups should designate one student to present the group's choice to the rest of the class and briefly defend that choice based on the information taken from their worksheets. Note: the group assigned to Spain has only one major figure—Philip II.

3. Allow half the class period for group discussion and completion of the worksheets and the other half for presentations.

4. Encourage students to use their textbooks to find facts to support their reasons for selecting a particular monarch.

5. After the groups complete the worksheet, ask them to take an informal group vote to determine their choice for the award.

6. Have members of the class comment on each group's choice, voicing agreement or disagreement, with an explanation of their opinions.

Name .... Date .... Class ....

History Simulation 19

HANDOUT MATERIAL

King or Queen for a Day—Worksheet

Complete the following worksheet as you discuss the actions, policies, and personal objectives of the absolute monarchs. Use the information to come to an agreement on who should receive the King- or Queen-for-a-Day award.

Monarchs to be Considered	
_____	_____
Political achievements		
Religious policy		
Military successes or failures		
Domestic policy		
Foreign policy		
Innovations during the monarch's rule		
State of the empire after the monarch's reign		

Choice for King- or Queen-for-a-Day award: _____

HISTORY SIMULATION 20

The Educational Contract

John Locke believed that people could use reason to devise a fair and workable form of government. In this activity, students use reason to understand the relationship between student and teacher.

TEACHER MATERIAL

Learning Objective To use reason to analyze the nature of the relationship between a teacher and students in a classroom.

Activity Students will work in groups of four to analyze the nature of the contract between a teacher and students. Students will first review Locke's theories about the nature of the contract between a government and the people. They will then discuss the rights and responsibilities of a teacher and students. Finally, students will formulate theories about the ideal educational contract.

Teacher Preparation Make a copy of the handout on page 40 for each student.

Activity Guidelines

1. Introduce the activity by reviewing John Locke's theories about the nature of the social contract between a government and the people, focusing on rights and responsibilities. Define *contract* as an agreement. Remind students that Locke used reasoned analysis to formulate his theories. Point out that one could also argue that an implied contract exists between a teacher and students in a classroom. Tell students that they will explore the nature of this contract and formulate their own theories about the ideal contract between a teacher and students.

2. Organize students into groups of four and give students a copy of the handout on page 40.

3. Give students time to discuss the questions provided on the handout. Suggest that each group appoint one person to record the group's ideas.

4. Have groups complete the chart and formulate their own theories about the ideal educational contract. Tell students that it is not necessary to have exactly five points in each box.

5. Have each group appoint a person to present the group's chart and theory to the entire class.

6. Discuss as a class the merits of each group's chart and theory. Then have students develop a new chart and theory using the best ideas from each group plus any ideas that came up during the discussion. Write the new chart and theory on the chalkboard.

7. Ask students to think about other relationships in their lives that involve spoken or unspoken contracts, such as parent/child, employers/employee, coach/player.
   - What are some of the rights and responsibilities associated with each of the parties in the contracts?
   - How do these contracts differ from the contract between a citizen and his or her government?

World History HISTORY SIMULATIONS

Name .... Date .... Class ....

History Simulation 20

HANDOUT MATERIAL

The Educational Contract

Group Discussion Questions

1. What rights do students in a classroom have? What rights does the teacher have?
2. What responsibilities do students in a classroom have? What responsibilities does the teacher have?
3. Who has the primary responsibility for how much an individual student learns—the teacher, the student, or both?
4. Is there an implied contract, or agreement, between the teacher and the students? What is the nature of the contract?
5. In an ideal classroom, what are the rights and responsibilities of the students and the teacher? What is the nature of the ideal contract between students and teachers?

Rights and Responsibilities

	Rights	**Responsibilities**
Teacher	1. _____ 2. _____ 3. _____ 4. _____ 5. _____	1. _____ 2. _____ 3. _____ 4. _____ 5. _____
Students	1. _____ 2. _____ 3. _____ 4. _____ 5. _____	1. _____ 2. _____ 3. _____ 4. _____ 5. _____

Theory of Educational Contract

The ideal contract between a teacher and students within a classroom is based on _____

_____

History Simulation 21

Unrest in Blaat
This activity will help students understand how conflicts can lead to revolution or civil unrest.

TEACHER MATERIAL

Learning Objective To develop an understanding of conflicts within a society that can lead to revolution or civil war.

Activity In groups, students will assume the roles of people in the imaginary country of Blaat. The roles are the king, the head of the official state religion, a rival preacher, a member of Parliament, and two citizens.

Teacher Preparation Make six copies of the handout material on page 42.

Activity Guidelines

1. Introduce the activity by explaining its objective. Briefly review the concepts of conflict and revolution. Then give students the following background information:

   Blaat is a country of about 10 million people. Its major industry is growing and exporting blueberries. Most of its citizens depend on the blueberry industry. King Borax of Blaat, who inherited the throne from his father, is an absolute monarch who believes he was given his power by God. One of his chief allies is Archbishop Ladlepate, head of the church. Both the king and the archbishop believe that in order for a country to be unified, there should be only one official religion.

   The king is currently engaged in a very costly war with Bordovia and needs to raise money—an additional 100 million klaams. Although the king is absolute monarch, there is a Parliament that meets at his request and authorizes new taxes and payments to the crown. Parliament often opposes the king's policies and, in the king's view, tries to interfere in government. Consequently, rather than call Parliament, King Borax instituted a tax on growers, pickers, and merchants of blueberries without the consent of Parliament. When citizens in the port city of Faavabin refused to pay the tax, King Borax closed the port and refused to allow any ships to come or go. Tons of blueberries lay rotting on the docks, and the people were outraged.

   When the opposition church leaders began preaching against these unfair measures, and against the war, King Borax had them imprisoned. The archbishop's men searched every church in the land and expelled opposition church leaders.

   However, when the country of Frangland entered the war and invaded the northern border of Blaat, King Borax was forced to call a session of Parliament to ask for money.

2. Organize the class into six groups. Assign one of the roles listed on the handout to each group. Explain to the groups that their job is to prepare a position statement from the role they have been assigned addressing the king's need to raise money.

3. Allow groups 30 minutes to reach a conclusion. Have each group appoint one member to write the position statement based on the group's stance.

4. Have a spokesperson from each group read the group's statement to the class.

5. Have students return to their groups to briefly consider and discuss the other groups' statements. Ask the groups to decide whether they should change their own stances based on the other groups' arguments and why.

World History — History Simulations 41

Name .... Date .... Class ....

History Simulation 21

HANDOUT MATERIAL

Unrest in Blaat

King Borax
You are God's lieutenant on earth. Like your father before you, you have absolute power given to you by God to pass any law you wish, and the people owe you unquestioning allegiance.

Archbishop Ladlepate
You have been chosen by God to lead the one true church. As such, you are the second most powerful person in Blaat. You owe your allegiance to King Borax. If he falls, so will you.

Lady Bolingreen
Your family has owned the great Bolingreen blueberry plantation for generations, since the days of good Queen Gertrude. Your family has always been loyal to the monarch, as have most of the great lords, but this king offends your honor. However, he is your king, and perhaps he is no worse than those fanatic opposition preachers who might replace him.

Master Scarford
You are a blueberry merchant of means, respected by your fellows. Your family has come a long way; just three generations ago, you were blueberry pickers on the Bolingreen plantation. But this king could drive you to bankruptcy with his taxes.

Preacher Baker
You are a preacher in the small opposition church in your county, and deeply committed to your religion. The archbishop and his men have tried to silence your preaching, even imprisoning you once, but you are determined to purify the Church of Blaat and establish the kingdom of God on earth.

Tamara Chattworth
You are a blueberry picker on the plantation of Lady Bolingreen, who is completely loyal to the king. You are a member of the opposition church. You have seven children to care for, and already the burden of taxes leaves you barely able to feed them.

42 History Simulations   World History

History Simulation 22

Where Do They Stand?

One of the reasons for France's difficulties during the late 1700s was the people's inability to reconcile the many different political opinions that existed. In this activity, students will examine a range of political opinions.

TEACHER MATERIAL

Learning Objective To understand change as reflected in leaders' political positions in the French Revolution.

Activity Students will form news teams to produce a television news special titled "Where Do They Stand?" They will interview leaders of the French Revolution who have differing views on the best path for France. To produce visuals for the television audience, students will create a chart based on the "Spectrum of Political Opinion" chart in their textbooks. In this new chart, students should indicate where the leader they have chosen to interview falls in the political spectrum and whether that person can best be described as (1) a radical, (2) a moderate, (3) a conservative, (4) a liberal, or (5) a reactionary. In preparing for the interviews, each news team will write a persuasive paragraph that summarizes its subject's position. Members of each team will also prepare interview questions that challenge the subject.

Teacher Preparation Copy the chart "Spectrum of Political Opinion" on page 569 of the Student Edition and enlarge it on a photocopy machine as a reference for students.

Activity Guidelines

1. Introduce the activity's objective and the steps involved. Post the "Spectrum of Political Opinion" so students can see it. Review with them the terms *radical, liberal, moderate, conservative, reactionary*. Point out that the political spectrum is also described in terms of position: radicals and liberals on the left, moderates in the middle, and conservatives and reactionaries on the right.

2. Organize the class into two groups and have students refer to the handout on page 44. Each group, or news team, will have 5 minutes to select one leader to interview (each group must pick a different person). The news teams will then meet to plan the following aspects of their news program:

   - Who will create the special's visual (an adaptation of the political opinion chart that reflects the group's additional information)?
   - Who will describe and summarize the subject's political position?
   - Who will portray the subject?
   - Who will conduct the interview?

   Each group also should assign a timekeeper and a record keeper. Remind students that all members of their news teams should be involved in the process of producing this special. Give students 5 minutes to select their subjects and 10 minutes to determine and assign individual team members' tasks.

3. After groups have selected leaders and tasks, allow 15 minutes to begin work, which will be completed in the next class. Suggest that the team writing the summary of the subject's political position outline their material or create a short list before actually writing the description.

4. At the second session, tell groups they have 30 minutes to complete their materials and 10 minutes for a dress rehearsal. Each group will then present its interview using the visuals it has created.

Name _____ Date _____ Class _____

History Simulation 22

HANDOUT MATERIAL

Where Do They Stand?

Select one of these individuals to be the subject of your interview:

- ☐ Louis XVI
- ☐ Maximilien Robespierre
- ☐ The Girondist leader
- ☐ One of the women who led the march for bread
- ☐ Napoleon Bonaparte
- ☐ George-Jacques Danton

Group Activity A
Draw your own version of the political opinion chart and any other visual materials you think would help your television special; fill in information on the chart as determined by your group.

Group Activity C
Create questions to ask the person you will interview.

Group Activity E
Select the news team who will conduct the interview.

Group Activity B
Write a description of the political position of the person your group selected to interview.

Individual Activity D
Select the person who acts as the political leader.

Individual Activity F
Select a timekeeper.

HISTORY SIMULATION 23

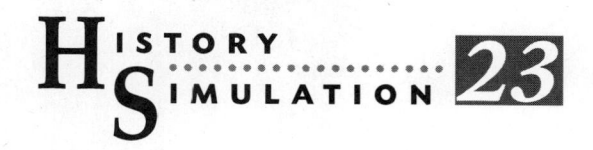

Pass It On!

The Industrial Revolution transformed forever the way people worked in factories. New ideas about how to improve efficiency, productivity, and profits abounded. Two of these new ideas were the division of labor and the assembly line.

TEACHER MATERIAL

Learning Objective To develop an understanding of division of labor and the assembly-line process and their effects on workers.

Activity In groups of five to nine, students will implement division of labor and the assembly-line process to produce memo pads. Groups will first meet to practice the tasks, determine who will complete each task, and establish a quota. All groups will then spend 10 minutes making memo pads. Within each group, each student will perform one task (see the task descriptions on the next page) and pass the material to the next worker. Finally, students will evaluate the experience in small-group and whole-class discussions.

Teacher Preparation Each group will need a supply of 8 1/2" x 11" paper (you may want to use scrap paper that is clean on one side), one or more rulers, pencils, scissors, staplers, access to a clock with a second hand, and a whistle or bell. Gather these materials and make one copy of the handout on page 46 for each student.

Activity Guidelines

1. Introduce the activity to students by explaining its objective and general steps. Briefly review the terms *division of labor* and *assembly line* and their importance in the 1800s and 1900s.

2. Organize students into groups of five to nine members for a 20-minute planning session. Give them the materials listed above. Distribute copies of the handout and briefly demonstrate each task on the form. Then instruct each group to read the task descriptions and try each of the first four tasks. Have them time one group member to see how many times he or she can repeat the task in 1 minute, working steadily and carefully. Then have students use the information to figure out about how many memo pads the group should be able to make in 10 minutes (remind students that they will lose a little time starting the process). Have students fill in the time and the total number of memo pads on the chart. Have students decide who will perform each task and write each student's name in the chart. Have them use the diagram to plan the group's seating arrangement.

3. Arrange for a 10-minute working session. When each group is prepared, direct the managers to start the production process.

4. Following the working session, have the small groups meet for a discussion. Ask the following questions: How did the process work? Did you meet your quota? Did each of you feel a sense of accomplishment? Why or why not? What other feelings did you have? Was the process more efficient than it might have been if each of you had performed all tasks, completely assembling one memo pad after another by yourself? Why or why not? Have groups discuss the questions, with one group member noting responses, which will then be reported to the class.

5. Finally, conduct a class discussion about the experience. Invite groups to share planning information and responses to the questions.

Name _____ Date _____ Class _____ World History

HISTORY SIMULATION 23

HANDOUT MATERIAL

Pass It On!

Planning Form/Group _____ **Product:** memo pads

Tasks	Worker's name	Number of times task is repeated
1. **Measurer** With a ruler, measure and draw lines dividing a piece of paper into four equal parts. Pass the paper to the Cutter.		
2. **Cutter** Cut the paper along the lines. Pass the pieces to the Counter.		
3. **Counter** Count 20 sheets and stack them. Pass the stack to the Stapler.		
4. **Stapler** Straighten the stack and staple it twice at the top edge. Put the finished product on an empty desk beside you.		
5. **Manager** Signal starting and stopping times with a bell or whistle. Supervise workers, making sure they work steadily, carefully, and quietly. Occasionally inspect the finished memo pads. Periodically time a worker for 1 minute to see if he or she is meeting the specified quota for that task.		

My group should be able to produce about _____ memo pads in 10 minutes.

```
    Measurer 1      Cutter 1       Counter 1      Stapler 1

Manager                    Table

    Measurer 2      Cutter 2       Counter 2      Stapler 2
```

(If two or more workers are completing the same task, have them sit facing one another.)

46   History Simulations

HISTORY SIMULATION 24

Through the Eyes of Artists
The transformation of the Western world during the 1700s and 1800s sparked new developments in all parts of society.

TEACHER MATERIAL

Learning Objective To develop an understanding of some of the major artistic movements that occurred during the 1700s and 1800s and their impact.

Activity Students will work in five groups representing each of the following artistic movements from the 1700s to the 1900s: romanticism, realism, symbolism, impressionism, and Postimpressionism. Groups will review the styles and philosophy of their specific art movements. Then they will consider how artists of that movement would react to some of the issues of the era and how they would convey their feelings and attitudes in their art. They will then form smaller groups of two to four to cooperate in creating essays, poems, short stories, plays, posters, murals, or other forms of art in the style of their movements. Following group work, students will meet as a class to share their project.

Teacher Preparation Groups will need poster board, paper for murals, and colored markers. Make one copy of the planning form on page 48 for each student.

Activity Guidelines

1. Introduce the activity to students by explaining its objective and general guidelines. Then briefly review the five art movements. Emphasize to students that artists in each of these movements had a definite point of view regarding society and the issues of the period and that they expressed their views in their art. You might cite, for example, Charles Dickens's handling of the plight of the lower classes in his novels and his views of conditions in debtors' prisons, factories, and hospitals. Distribute copies of the worksheet. Tell students that this worksheet may help them organize their planning for this activity.

2. Allow students to form five groups, one for each movement. Have groups meet for 5 to 10 minutes to discuss the point of view that members of their movement might bring to specific social and political issues studied in this chapter. Possible subjects include emigration, urbanization, city life, utopia, city parks, communism, the significance of the germ theory, and Freudian psychology. Students should also discuss the artistic style the artists would use to portray specific subjects.

3. Organize the five groups into subgroups of two to four students. Groups should organize according to modes of expression, such as poetry, posters, murals, essays, short stories, or other art forms. Urge these groups to brainstorm a list of possible topics and then select one. Then allow students at least 15–20 minutes to plan their projects. Emphasize that their work should be in the style of the movement they represent. Most students will need to complete their projects at home.

4. The next class period, have each group identify the movement it represents and read or display its project. Have students respond to what they see in the different projects.

5. Then ask students to compare the representation of society and politics by the different art movements. How do they think the artistic rendering of these themes may have affected the public's attitudes? Do they think the art movements grew out of the events of the period, or did the movements shape events?

Name .... Date .... Class ....

History Simulation 24

HANDOUT MATERIAL

Through the Eyes of Artists—Worksheet

Movement (check one):

☐ Romanticism   ☐ Realism   ☐ Symbolism   ☐ Impressionism   ☐ Postimpressionism

1. Objective of the movement:
_____
_____

2. Artistic style of the movement:
_____
_____

3. Attitude toward society, culture, politics:
_____
_____
_____
_____

4. Subject or themes for exploration:
_____
_____

Choose the mode for exploring your topic:

☐ Mural
☐ Short story
☐ Play
☐ Poster
☐ Essay
☐ Poetry
☐ Other _____

48   History Simulations   World History

# HISTORY SIMULATION 25

Charting a Course... Again!

Reformers in Great Britain during the 1800s faced obstacles in trying to change the political system. This activity allows students to work together to try to win public support for reforms advocated by the Chartists.

TEACHER MATERIAL

Learning Objective To develop an understanding of the challenges that confronted political reformers during the 1800s.

Activity Students will take on the roles of leaders of the Chartists. The time is the 1830s just following the rejection by the British Parliament of the Chartists' second petition (signed by more than three million people), which called for major political changes. Students will assess the situation of the Chartists, establish new goals for them, and plan a publicity campaign to accomplish these goals.

Teacher Preparation Students will need art materials (poster board, colored markers, rulers) appropriate for developing a publicity campaign. Make a copy of the planning form on page 50 for each student.

Activity Guidelines

1. Introduce the activity by explaining the objective and the general steps students are to complete. Briefly review the Chartist reform movement, emphasizing that although the Chartists had great support among the working class, they were unable to translate that support into political power to achieve their ends. Remind students that during this period (1838–1848) workers could not vote. Hence, even with massive support by fellow laborers, they could not pressure Parliament into action. Stress that students' planning must somehow get around this obstacle and bring real political clout to bear on Parliament.

2. Students should first meet as a class. Have them discuss the predicament of the Chartist movement to be sure they all understand the circumstances. Then have students brainstorm potential political allies, such as the middle class, disenfranchised women, members of Parliament, or even aristocrats who feel threatened by the middle class.

3. When students have identified a likely ally, tell them to analyze this group and to list reasons this group might consider cooperating with the Chartists. Then have students list reasons the group might be opposed to cooperating with the Chartists.

4. After students have completed their analyses, have them brainstorm strategies for enlisting the help of their targeted ally. These strategies might include a direct-mail campaign, speeches, posters or billboards, or a newspaper campaign. Students should limit their strategies to those available in the 1800s. Have students select several strategies and form committees, each taking responsibility for one strategy. Allow the class 20–30 minutes to accomplish this stage of the activity.

5. After students have finished planning, allow a 30-minute work period during the next class. Have each committee proceed with implementing its strategy. Emphasize that efforts need not be in revised, final form.

6. Following the work session, have students briefly share their results. Then discuss the activity with the students. Ask them to consider these questions:
    - How expensive would their strategy be?
    - Would the working-class organization have been able to afford it?
    - Would this strategy appeal to their targeted ally?
    - Does their brief experience with this activity give them clues as to why the Chartist movement may have faded?

World History — History Simulations

Name .... Date .... Class ....

HISTORY SIMULATION 25

HANDOUT MATERIAL

Charting a Course . . . Again!

Chartist Goal	Targeted Group	Characteristics of Targeted Group

Why this group might

Support Chartists' efforts	Not support Chartists' efforts

Committee Assignment _____

Arguments for Gaining Support of Targeted Group

1. Arguments to demonstrate interests shared by Chartists and the targeted group:
   _____
   _____

2. Arguments for overcoming targeted group's opposition to alliance:
   _____
   _____

3. What action should the individual take who reads or hears the campaign message?
   _____
   _____

HISTORY SIMULATION 26

Power Plays

The desire for national independence, known as nationalism, became one of the most powerful forces at work in Europe during the 1800s. In some cases it led to the unification of several kingdoms into one country. In others it led to the breaking apart of old empires. Whether peaceful or violent, however, nationalist movements always included many different groups trying to further their own interests.

TEACHER MATERIAL

Learning Objective To demonstrate an understanding of how various social classes will have differing opinions of a country's need for reform and differing methods for bringing about (or preventing) change.

Activity Students form groups representing the monarchy, nobility, the middle class, workers, and peasants. Using the handout on page 52, students identify the goals, concerns, and ideas of the class they represent. Groups then consider how these goals will be achieved and what action will be taken. Afterward, groups report their decisions to the rest of the class.

Teacher Preparation Provide a copy of page 52 for each group.

Activity Guidelines

1. Introduce the activity by explaining its objective and discussing the interrelations among these different classes. Briefly review the political and social ideas—both old and new—that were prevalent in Europe during the 1800s. Old ideas included the divine right of kings to rule and the belief in the hierarchy of nature (one's place in life is determined by birth, and to transgress this law of nature and God is a crime). New ideas included the desire for freedom from oppression, the belief in individual rights, and the belief in the right to self-determination of nations and representative government.

2. Organize the class into five groups: monarchy, nobility, middle class, workers, and peasants. Distribute one handout to each group. A description of each class is provided.

3. Have group members work together to identify and address political, social, and economic objectives using the information on the handout.

4. Allow 10 to 15 minutes for each group to review its objectives. Groups should then consider the methods available in meeting their objectives. The advantages and disadvantages of each method should then be listed under the appropriate heading.

5. Each group develops a plan of action describing their proposed response.

6. Groups report to the class their decisions, how they came to their conclusions, why they chose a specific path, and what form their plan of action will take.

Name .... Date .... Class ....

History Simulation 26

HANDOUT MATERIAL

Power Plays—Developing a Plan of Action

Classes

Peasants
- agricultural
- illiterate
- most oppressed class
- largest population
- only access to power structure is through its size and necessary economic role

Workers
- industrial
- mostly illiterate
- oppressed
- next largest population
- access to power structure is through its size and economic role

Middle Class
- business owners, students, intellectuals
- mostly literate
- somewhat oppressed
- outnumbers the monarchy and nobility
- access to power structure through dissemination of ideas and economic role

Nobility
- landowners who possess much of the wealth
- literate
- exploits lower classes
- very small population
- the power class that looks after the monarch's and its own interests

Monarchy
- lawmaker, possesses great wealth and absolute control
- exploits all other classes
- consists of one person

Class: _____

Objectives (political, social, economic)	Methods of Meeting Objectives (include advantages and disadvantages)	Proposed Plan of Action

52   History Simulations   World History

HISTORY SIMULATION 27

The Imperial Press

During the late 1800s, when the United States became involved in the imperialistic scramble for territory, a new kind of newspaper reporting arose known as yellow journalism. Featuring huge headlines and melodramatic stories, the yellow press twisted facts in order to influence public opinion and attract readers.

TEACHER MATERIAL

Learning Objective To gain an appreciation for the role of the yellow press in the Age of Imperialism.

Activity Students will work in four groups to complete a four-page newspaper, *The Imperial Press*, covering life in the Age of Imperialism. Each group will create a different page: a front page, a national news page, an editorial page, and a human-interest page. The activity will take two class periods, and students will be required to meet the deadline for a completed mock-up page by the end of the second period. Members of the four groups will spend the first half of the first period assigning responsibilities and brainstorming ideas. The second half of the first period will be spent completing rough drafts of articles, cartoons, ads, design layouts, and anything else of interest. During the first half of the second period, the groups will edit, redesign, and polish their materials. The last half of the second period will be used to paste up the final product on poster board.

Teacher Preparation Have students bring to class daily newspapers and spend a few minutes discussing their elements and relating them to the paper the students will create. Note, for instance, that since the students represent an American press, the front-page stories and pictures should relate directly to the United States (perhaps the Spanish-American War or Matthew C. Perry). Students will also need a copy of the handout on page 54, poster board, paste, scissors, and rulers. They may wish to use colored pencils and markers.

Activity Guidelines

1. Introduce the activity with the daily newspapers as the main example. Explain the overall objective of the assignment and stress the importance of cooperation in meeting a deadline.

2. Organize students into four groups and tell them to assign the following roles to group members:
   - editors, who have final say on information included and responsibility for grammar and spelling
   - reporters, who write and edit stories to fit the plan
   - designers, in charge of mastheads, borders, and visuals as well as placement of the final design on poster board
   - cartoonists, who provide editorial cartoons

   Tell students to decide what is most appropriate for their pages and have them double check with the other groups to make sure that information is not repeated.

3. After groups have assigned activities and brainstormed ideas, have students work in pairs or separately to complete the first drafts of individual tasks.

4. At the start of the second day, tell students to spend the first half of the period finalizing their work and making necessary corrections. Give them a deadline. Tell them they must then stop editing and put the final page onto poster board.

Name .... Date .... Class ....

History Simulation 27

HANDOUT MATERIAL

The Imperial Press—Worksheet

Use the following worksheet to plan your page of *The Imperial Press*. Work as a group to make decisions about assignments and information to include. Record the name of each group member according to the job he or she selects. You should also refer to the list of steps included as you plan and keep track of your time schedule and deadline. Check off each box when the task is complete.

Editors	**Reporters**	**Designers**	**Cartoonists**
_____	_____	_____	_____
_____	_____	_____	_____
_____	_____	_____	_____
_____	_____	_____	_____

1
- ☐ Decide on stories, visuals, and so on to include on the page.
- ☐ Check with other groups to make sure no story or visual is duplicated.

If you find another group that wants to use the same material, you will have to decide where that material best belongs for the overall good of the newspaper.

2
Begin the tasks your group has assigned to its members:
- ☐ Write stories or editorials
- ☐ Make visuals
- ☐ Draw cartoons
- ☐ Create a rough layout for the page

3
When tasks are completed:
- ☐ Review
- ☐ Rewrite and redesign as necessary until it is time to go to press.

4
At press time your group must stop editing and rewriting and begin pasting the final product on poster board.

Press Time Deadline

Day _____

Hour _____

54   History Simulations   World History

History Simulation 28

In the Trenches

A new and terrible kind of war, known as trench warfare, arose during World War I. Soldiers lived in trenches for weeks at a time. In addition to fighting the enemy, they had to endure cold, mud, rats, lice, and disease.

TEACHER MATERIAL

Learning Objective To develop an appreciation for and an understanding of what fighting, especially trench warfare, was like during World War I.

Activity In two groups (Allied Powers and Central Powers) students will apply the conditions of war through movement on a game board, drawing cards (each of which details a situation and a consequence) and forfeiting troops. Students will take turns representing their sides for one move. Next, each group will meet separately to discuss and evaluate what they learned.

Teacher Preparation You will need one die, two big boxes of toothpicks (200 total), two player tokens from any board game, and a sheet of heavy construction paper approximately 20" x 20". "In the Trenches" is played on a board of 20 squares drawn on the perimeter of the construction paper. Prepare the game board as follows: Draw a "track" around the outside edge of the board, with a large space in each corner and five spaces along each side. Label one corner "Hospital" and divide it in half with a diagonal line; label one-half "visitor" and one-half "patient." Label another corner "start." Along each side label one space "Wounded: Go to Hospital" and another three spaces "Battle!" Finally, label any two blank spaces "Shuffle." Make a copy of the cards sheet on page 56 and cut out the cards. Place the Battle cards face-down in the middle of the board. Place the game board on a table around which everyone can gather.

Activity Guidelines

1. Introduce the activity by explaining its objective and general procedure. Briefly review the countries fighting on each side, trench warfare, and the term *stalemate*.

2. Organize students into two groups, the Allied Powers and the Central Powers. Lay out the game board on the table. Give each group 100 toothpicks. Tell them that each toothpick represents 10,000 soldiers, for a total of 1 million soldiers per side.

3. Explain that if a player lands on the Hospital square, he or she is just visiting. A player becomes a patient there if a card requires it or if he or she lands on a Wounded: Go to Hospital space. Then explain to students that disease takes its toll on hospitalized troops. For a player to leave the hospital, he or she must roll a 1, 3, or 5. Players rolling a 2, 4, or 6 lose 2,000, 4,000, or 6,000 troops and lose a turn.

4. Have each side take turns throwing the die and moving the marker. Students landing on a "Battle!" space draw a card. They should then follow the directions on the card (the BIG PICTURE cards require both sides to follow directions). Lost troops are piled upon the board. If a student lands on a "Shuffle" space or if the entire deck has been turned over, the cards are reshuffled and play resumes. Play continues until one army is wiped out or elects to surrender.

5. Have each group meet separately to discuss what they learned. During this time, write the following discussion questions on the chalkboard: (1) Compare the perspectives of a soldier in the trenches to those of a general who gives attack and retreat orders from behind the lines. How does each evaluate cost and gain? (2) What does it mean to win a battle in trench warfare? (3) What do you think was the hardest thing a soldier had to endure? Then hold a class discussion of the questions.

World History · History Simulations · 55

Name .... Date .... Class ....

History Simulation 28

HANDOUT MATERIAL

In the Trenches

YOU ARE THERE:
You've got so many lice, your clothes are crawling with them. But killing them gives you something to do while being shelled.
- Lose 10,000 troops.

YOU ARE THERE:
Poison gas you have launched blows back over your own troops. Two friends didn't get their masks on in time.
- Lose 20,000 troops.

YOU ARE THERE:
Rats eat last night's rations you were saving. Go hungry.
- Lose 10,000 troops.

YOU ARE THERE:
You're lying facedown in mud trying to get back to your trench. Bullets whiz over your head. You notice a shell crater and roll in.
- Lose a turn.

YOU ARE THERE:
Nights are cold and wet. Two of your toes get frostbitten. Go to the hospital.
- Lose 10,000 troops.

YOU ARE THERE:
Supplies didn't make it through the lines. You are being shelled but must wait for more ammo and go hungry until supplies arrive.
- Lose 30,000 troops.

YOU ARE THERE:
Barbed wire cuts your hand. It's so infected you can't operate a gun. Go to the hospital until you're recalled to duty.
- Lose 10,000 troops.

YOU ARE THERE:
Dug in, you sit under heavy fire. The roar of impact has made your ears bleed.
- Lose 10,000 troops.

YOU ARE THERE:
In a rare lull, you and a comrade take advantage of the quiet and share whispered memories of home.

THE BIG PICTURE:
Tannenburg Allied cost: 30,000 dead/92,000 prisoners; Central cost: 13,000 dead.
- You have no gun to fight with. Pick one up from your comrades who fell before you.

THE BIG PICTURE:
Ypres Allied cost: 60,000 dead; Central cost: 130,000 dead.
- Poison gas is introduced here. Everyone panics trying to escape. You see thousands die, gasping for air.

THE BIG PICTURE:
Verdun Allied cost: 375,000 dead; Central cost: 375,000 dead.
- For nearly two years both sides make countless attacks and retreats. The front moves fewer than 10 miles.

THE BIG PICTURE:
The Somme Allied cost: 200,000 dead; Central cost: 175,000 dead.
- Tanks are introduced here, but they cannot cross the trenches. You see one hit directly. Everyone inside is burned.

THE BIG PICTURE:
At Sea Allied cost: 50,000 dead; Central cost: 20,000 dead.
- Blockades by both sides make supplies at the front and at home scarce. Your rations are cut in half.

THE BIG PICTURE:
Belgian Campaign Allied cost: 100,000 dead; Central cost: 50,000 dead.
- You see men from your own unit beating civilians and looting. One of them is shot by a sniper.

THE BIG PICTURE:
Outside Paris Allied cost: 70,000 dead; Central cost: 120,000 dead.
- To protect Paris, taxicabs are requisitioned to transport troops into position. Escaping Parisians clog the roads.

THE BIG PICTURE:
The Marne Allied cost: 110,000 dead; Central cost: 140,000 dead.
- This is the war's first Allied victory. But all that really means is that you won't be home by Christmas after all.

THE BIG PICTURE:
Passchendaele Allied cost: 210,000 dead; Central cost: 270,000 dead.
- Neither side understands why the enemy (a valiant but inferior fighting force) hasn't crumbled.

History Simulations   World History

# HISTORY SIMULATION 29

The Postwar World

The postwar era brought economic difficulties and political problems to many nations. In addition, artists and intellectuals became disillusioned with traditional means of expression and began searching for something new. In this activity, students combine their knowledge of postwar problems with their understanding of the newly emerging means of expression.

TEACHER MATERIAL

Learning Objective To deepen understanding of the people and problems of the postwar world.

Activity Students will work in groups to create original works of literature that express positions on postwar issues or events. Each group will review 10 settings and subjects, choose one, establish a position, and create a work that communicates that position.

Teacher Preparation Copy page 58 for each student.

Activity Guidelines

1. Introduce the activity by explaining the objective and general steps. Briefly review that some artists and writers of the postwar era addressed social issues and problems in their works. Remind students that artistic expression was controlled in some societies.

2. Organize students into small groups and distribute copies of page 58. Have each group choose a subject. Point out that they should consider the setting (time and place) as they make their choices. For example, a group that chooses item 10 should recall that artists and writers in the Soviet Union were expected to glorify Soviet achievements in their works. Point out, however, that the group may choose to disregard that expectation, as did some actual artists and writers. Point out, too, that some subjects are more general than others. A group choosing item 4 might focus on the effects of inflation on a middle-class German family and on what it expects the government to do. In addition, suggest that students consider point of view. A group choosing item 5 may opt to write from a coal miner's perspective or from the viewpoint of a coal company. Finally, point out the means of expression offered for each item. Encourage students not to shy away from creating a song; they may write new lyrics to a familiar tune.

3. Next, direct each group to: (a) review the items, discussing the setting, subject, and possible positions and means of expression (students may want to choose a group leader to direct the discussion); (b) choose an item and review the text dealing with the subject (students may do additional research to learn more); (c) establish a position (viewpoint); and (d) collaborate on an original work.

4. After groups have finished, have them present their works. Conduct a follow-up discussion, writing on the chalkboard and discussing responses to the following questions:

   - Did the work accurately portray what we know of the time and place?
   - Was the position on the subject clear?
   - What was the point of view?
   - What techniques did the creators of each work use to express their positions?

World History

History Simulations

Name .... Date .... Class ....

History Simulation 29

HANDOUT MATERIAL

The Postwar World

1. **Setting:** The United States in the 1930s
   Subject: direct relief from the federal government
   Position: _____
   Means of Expression: song, poem, or essay

2. **Setting:** Italy in 1924
   Subject: Mussolini's dictatorship
   Position: _____
   Means of Expression: poem, short story, one-act play, or song

3. **Setting:** the United States in 1919
   Subject: membership in the League of Nations
   Position: _____
   Means of Expression: song or essay

4. **Setting:** Germany in 1923
   Subject: inflation
   Position: _____
   Means of Expression: song, poem, or essay

5. **Setting:** Great Britain in 1926
   Subject: general strike
   Position: _____
   Means of Expression: poem, song, one-act play, or short story

6. **Setting:** Germany in the late 1930s
   Subject: Hitler's policies toward German Jews
   Position: _____
   Means of Expression: poem, short story, one-act play, or song

7. **Setting:** France in 1936
   Subject: the Popular Front
   Position: _____
   Means of Expression: song, poem, or essay

8. **Setting:** the Soviet Union in the late 1920s
   Subject: collectivization
   Position: _____
   Means of Expression: song, poem, short story, or one-act play

9. **Setting:** Italy in 1921
   Subject: actions of the Blackshirts
   Position: _____
   Means of Expression: song, poem, essay, one-act play, or short story

10. **Setting:** the Soviet Union in 1935
    Subject: a Soviet artist's life
    Position: _____
    Means of Expression: song, poem, story, or one-act play

58 History Simulations World History

History Simulation 30

What's My Name?

The period between the two world wars was a time of struggle for many colonial peoples who desired their independence. The spirit of nationalism that rocked Europe in the 1800s swept through Asia, Africa, and Latin America in the 1920s and 1930s.

TEACHER MATERIAL

Learning Objective To identify key individuals in a country's fight for independence.

Activity Three teams of students will compete in *What's My Name?* They will identify leaders in nations struggling for their independence. Information will be taken from Chapter 30.

Teacher Preparation Each team will need index cards on which to write several clues for each person selected, as well as a copy of page 60 for each team member.

Activity Guidelines

1. Introduce the activity to students by explaining the objective and the steps. Briefly review the issue of nationalism after World War I: During the postwar years, many countries wanting to be free from foreign influence and internal autocratic domination struggled to establish their independence.

2. Arrange students in three teams. Each group will choose a captain, a scorekeeper, and a reader. The captain acts as timekeeper, collects the clues written by the team, and checks to make sure that the clues are written correctly. The scorekeeper keeps score while the game is played. The reader reads aloud each team's clues during the game.

3. Each team will review parts of Chapter 30: Team 1 reviews Section 1; Team 2 reviews Sections 2 and 4; and Team 3 reviews Sections 3 and 5. As the teams review the material, they should identify people who played key roles. Each team then creates a statement that gives clues to the person chosen. For example, for Franklin D. Roosevelt, the clue might be: "I liked the idea that my nation would be a good neighbor to other countries." Caution students not to create obscure clues that no one will be able to solve. Each clue should be written on an index card with the speaker's name on the back. After 30 minutes, the captain calls time, collects the cards, and makes sure that each card lists the clue and the speaker.

4. Each team captain counts how many clues the team has; all teams should start with the same number of clues. Then the reader, starting with Team 1, reads the clues to the other teams. The members of each team confer, and the first team to get the correct answer scores one point. If after one minute no one has answered correctly, the reader should announce the correct answer. No points are awarded. The team that has the most points after all clues have been read is the winner.

Name .... Date .... Class ....

HISTORY SIMULATION 30

HANDOUT MATERIAL

What's My Name? Planning Form

1. **Decision Making** Choose a team captain, a scorekeeper, and a reader. The captain will keep track of the time allowed for writing the clues—30 minutes. The captain collects the cards and makes sure that they are prepared correctly. The captain also counts the clues and compares the number with those of the other teams. All teams should start with the same number of clues. There should be one statement on the front of each card; the statement's speaker should be on the back. The reader will read the clues to the other teams. The scorekeeper will keep score.

Team Captain	Reader	Scorekeeper
_____	_____	_____

2. **Individual Work** Review your particular section of Chapter 30—Team 1 reviews Section 1, Team 2 reviews Sections 2 and 4, Team 3 reviews Sections 3 and 5. As you read the material, note below the people who played a role in events.

Key People from Section _____

_____ _____ _____
_____ _____ _____
_____ _____ _____
_____ _____ _____
_____ _____ _____

3. **Group Work** Create statements that might have been spoken by key people from the chapter. There should be one statement on each card, with the name of the speaker on the other side.

4. **Playing the Game** Begin with Team 1. The reader reads a statement; the other teams should respond with the correct speaker. If, after one minute, neither team has identified the speaker correctly, the reader announces the correct answer. No points are awarded. Each team's scorekeeper keeps track of correct responses. Play then rotates to the other two teams. At the end of the game, after all the clues have been read, the scorekeepers tell how many correct answers each team got.

HISTORY SIMULATION 31

The Path to War

In the 1930s totalitarian regimes came to power in Europe and Asia. The Western democracies were uneasy about these developments, but despite their fears, they could not cooperate enough to provide for their collective security.

TEACHER MATERIAL

Learning Objective To demonstrate an understanding of the Western democracies' responses to key events at the beginning of World War II.

Activity Students work in 12 pairs or small groups to review the chapter to find facts that explain how various Western nations responded to the actions of other nations in the days leading to World War II. Students then categorize these responses as *action* or *nonaction,* and then share the information by writing it on a class chart.

Teacher Preparation Make one copy of page 62 for each group. Have ten index cards ready to give to each group (120 cards). Hang a large piece of chart paper where everyone can see it. Ask several students to print the names of the following countries on the paper, leaving enough space under each name to write five sentences or so: Germany, Japan, China, Italy, Ethiopia, Spain, the Soviet Union, Denmark, Luxembourg, the Netherlands, Belgium, Great Britain, and the United States.

Activity Guidelines

1. Explain the learning objective and give a general description of the activity.

2. Briefly review the world situation in the 1930s: Totalitarian forces rose to power in Europe and Asia. Great Britain, France, and the United States witnessed the aggressive actions of Japan, Italy, and Germany but could not always agree on how to respond to these actions. In some cases, the Western powers decided not to act (*nonaction*). In other cases, they took strong, well-planned actions.

3. Organize the class into 12 small groups or pairs. Assign each group a number between 1 and 12. Explain that the group numbers correspond to the numbered statements on the student handout.

4. Have groups select one member to be the captain and another to be the recorder. If a group has more than two members, all others will be fact-finders who review their textbooks for facts that relate to the numbered statements. The captain appoints members to keep track of time, collects the fact cards, and makes sure that only one fact is recorded on each card.

5. As the captain reads each card, the group decides if the response was an *action* or a *nonaction* and marks the cards *A* or *N*. After groups have classified the responses, they should come to a consensus about which five responses were most important. They will record these five responses on the class chart. Groups have 30 minutes to do this step.

6. When students have filled out the cards, gather the class together. Ask the recorders from all the groups to present the information they found by writing the fact and *A* or *N* from their cards on the chart paper under the appropriate country's name. Then have one member of the group explain why the country responded the way it did.

7. After all the groups have recorded their responses to their statement, have them participate in a class discussion about how the Western democracies responded to the events leading up to 1939. Ask students if they think that war could have been prevented and, if so, how. After groups have completed the activity, they should better understand the nature of Western responses to events at the beginning of World War II.

Name _____ Date _____ Class _____

HISTORY SIMULATION 31

HANDOUT MATERIAL

The Path to War—Action or Nonaction Planning Form

1. Japan demonstrates its territorial ambitions by expanding into Manchuria and setting up a puppet ruler.
2. Italian forces invade Ethiopia.
3. Spanish Civil War provides an opportunity for Hitler to test his war machine.
4. Hitler occupies the Rhineland.
5. Hitler and Mussolini sign the Rome-Berlin Axis.
6. Germany annexes Austria.
7. Stalin begins secret talks with Hitler.
8. German transports attack Denmark and the Low Countries.
9. Churchill delivers his first speech as prime minister to the House of Commons.
10. Germans begin blitz of London.
11. The U.S. Congress passes laws to prevent American involvement in the war.
12. The Japanese government announces plans for "a new order in greater East Asia."

Decision Making Choose a captain and a recorder. All other students are fact-finders. On each index card, write one response relating to your statement. The group leader will keep track of the time for reviewing the material and writing the facts—30 minutes. The recorder enters the information onto the class chart.

Captain _____   **Recorder** _____

Fact-Finders _____

Individual Work Review Chapter 31. Below, write the responses that countries made that relate to your topic.

_____
_____
_____

Group Work: Action or Nonaction?
Your team will write one response on each card. When your leader calls time, hand the cards to your leader. Your leader will read the cards aloud. Decide if the responses involve action or nonaction and then write A or N on the card.

History Simulation 32

What Am I?

This activity engages students in the process of working together to review significant events, people, and places related to changes in North America and Europe during the cold war.

TEACHER MATERIAL

Learning Objective To demonstrate an understanding of the events, people, and places connected with the cold war.

Activity Two teams of students will choose events, people, or places to be acted out in a game of charades. These subjects will be based on facts from Chapter 32, including captions and special features. Each team will meet to develop subject cards. Then the teams will meet as one group and set guidelines for playing, such as permissible hand signals for small words like *the*. The game can then begin.

Teacher Preparation Provide a three-minute timer, two index cards for each student, and one copy of page 64 for each team.

Activity Guidelines

1. Explain to the students that they will be playing a game of charades based on facts from this chapter.

2. Organize the class into Team A and Team B. Give each team one student handout and each student two index cards.

3. Give each team 15 minutes to develop subjects for the other team to act out. They should try to make these subjects challenging in order to stump the other team. Have each team member write two subjects, one on each card. Tell each team to pick someone to check all the cards to be sure that there are no duplicates. Then have students assign a recorder and a timekeeper for each team.

4. When the cards have been completed, the teams should meet to decide the game guidelines. The team recorder will write down on the student handout sheet the rules the group has set. Each team recorder will also alert the opposing team during the game when they are not following these rules.

5. Allow half a class period to play charades. Each round lasts three minutes. One member of Team A gives a card to any member of Team B, who reads it silently and then acts out the subject for the rest of Team B to guess. If Team B members cannot guess, play goes to the other team and no points are scored. If Team B does guess the subject, a point is scored and another subject card is given to a second member of Team B to act out. If a subject is still being acted out when the round ends, that subject is discarded. Rounds should begin with alternating teams: Team A should go first in rounds 1, 3, and 5, and Team B should go first in rounds 2, 4, and 6.

6. Play continues until one team has acted out all of the other team's subjects, or until the end of the sixth round. (You may extend play to 8 or 10 rounds if you wish.) The team with the higher score wins.

Name .... Date .... Class ....

History Simulation 32

HANDOUT MATERIAL

What Am I?—Guidelines and Score Sheet

Sample Subject: The Berlin Airlift

Game Guidelines:

No speaking

_____   _____
_____   _____
_____   _____
_____   _____
_____   _____
_____   _____

SCORE SHEET

Team _____

Round 1	Round 2	Round 3

Round 4	Round 5	Round 6

Final Score _____

64   History Simulations   World History

HISTORY SIMULATION 33

Facts on Asia: A Cause-Effect Game

This activity employs a game-show format to review the relationships among the major events in Asia and the Pacific since 1945.

TEACHER MATERIAL

Learning Objective To demonstrate an understanding of change, conflict, nationalism, and cultural diffusion in Asia and the Pacific from World War II to the present.

Activity Small groups of students will prepare selections in various categories for a game in which players are given an effect and must supply the matching cause. Then teams of students will play the game.

Teacher Preparation Make one copy of the handout material on page 66 for each student. Students will need scissors to cut out the notecards on the handout. (You may prefer to have them use a supply of index cards since they will be more durable.) The timekeeper will need access to a clock with a second hand, preferably one that is visible to the entire class.

Activity Guidelines

1. Introduce the activity to students by explaining its objective and general steps.

2. Have the class choose a timekeeper, a scorekeeper, and a host. Organize the class into six groups, one for each category on the handout.

3. Tell the six groups to use information from Chapter 33 to create a list of at least eight effects per group. Remind them to keep to the chapter's major points and to avoid asking questions about trivial information. Allow 15 minutes for this part of the activity. Emphasize that each group is responsible for the cards it submits and will be called on to make a decision if a player gives a response that is not listed on the card but might be acceptable.

4. Tell students first to write the effect on the card in capital letters, then an acceptable cause below the effect, and finally the name of the category on the back of the card. At the end of 15 minutes, have each group submit its cards to the host, who keeps six separate piles.

5. Organize the class into two teams. Make sure that members from each group are on each team. (In case a question arises about the acceptability of a response, there will be at least one group member on the opposite team able to decide.)

6. The host reads to the first player an effect in any category other than the one that the player's group created. The player responds with the cause in that category. The timekeeper should allow 15 seconds for each response. If a cause is not given in time, the card is returned to the bottom of the pile for that category. Each correct response scores two points. An incorrect response subtracts two points. Play rotates from team to team, with team members taking turns as players, until just before the class period ends.

7. Just before the end of class, ask students which categories or topics they found difficult. Encourage them to review those sections of the chapter before the chapter test is given.

Name .... Date .... Class ....

HISTORY SIMULATION 33

HANDOUT MATERIAL

Facts on Asia: A Cause-Effect Game

Check the box next to your group's category:

- ☐ Independence movements
- ☐ Communist gains
- ☐ Cultural exchanges
- ☐ Cold war upheaval
- ☐ Forming democracies
- ☐ New economic roles

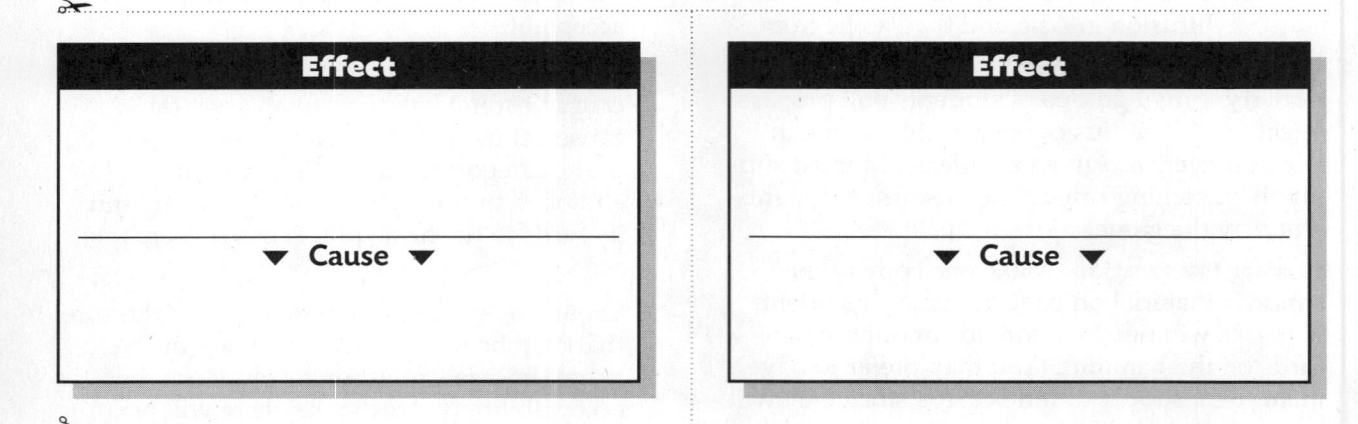

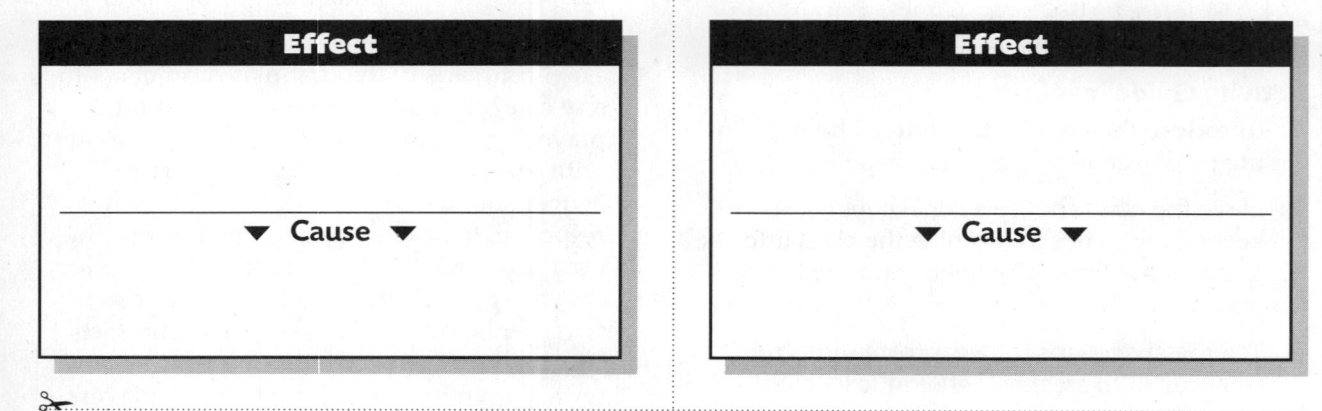

Effect

▼ Cause ▼

Effect

▼ Cause ▼

Effect

▼ Cause ▼

Effect

▼ Cause ▼

Effect

▼ Cause ▼

Effect

▼ Cause ▼

History Simulations

World History

HISTORY SIMULATION 34

Creating National Unity

By most estimates, there are at least 3,000 different ethnic groups on the continent of Africa. Africans speak more than 1,000 languages, and fewer than 50 of these languages are spoken by more than 100,000 people. This diversity made the issue of national unity—let alone Pan-Africanism—one of the most difficult problems that newly independent nations faced.

TEACHER MATERIAL

Learning Objective To demonstrate how difficult and complex it is to build a sense of unity among diverse people.

Activity Students will declare their class an independent nation. Their task will be to develop a sense of national unity that is based on common goals and values but that also respects individual differences.

Teacher Preparation Make one copy of the handout material on page 68 for each group.

Activity Guidelines

1. Review with students what is meant by nationalism and national identity. Have students link the concepts with the information on newly independent African states discussed in Chapter 34.

2. Tell students that their class has been given the status of an independent nation. It is their task to work together to develop a sense of unity among themselves, in much the same way that newly independent nations had to develop their own national identities.

3. Organize the class into groups of four or five students. Each group will develop a proposal on how the identity of their "nation" should be defined. Encourage students to seek ways to balance their diversity and personal differences with common goals and values.

4. Along with their proposal, each group will create a symbol or other representation of their idea of national unity. For example, they might create:
   - a national flag that represents both the unity and the diversity of the class.
   - a national icon (like Uncle Sam) that has relevance to the class.
   - a national anthem whose style and lyrics reflect the class.

5. After the groups have completed their proposals and symbols, reassemble the class to form a Congress. Each group will choose a spokesperson to present their proposal and symbol to the Congress.

6. After the spokespeople have made their presentations, allow them to debate the merits and drawbacks of each proposal in an effort to arrive at a consensus.

7. Hold a national referendum, allowing each member of the class to vote on the proposals and symbols he or she believes best define the national identity of the class. Then discuss the results with the class. If students have voted overwhelmingly for one proposal, point out that a high degree of "nationalism" has taken hold of the class. If, on the other hand, the votes indicate no clear consensus, draw parallels between conflicts within the class and those within newly independent African nations.

8. Ask students to evaluate the exercise. You may wish to as questions such as the following:
   - How difficult was it for the group to decide what its members had in common?
   - What additional challenges might a newly liberated nation face in developing a sense of national unity and identity?
   - How important are national symbols in creating a sense of national identity and unity?

Name .... Date .... Class ....

History Simulation 34

HANDOUT MATERIAL

Creating National Unity

Similarities	Differences
Examples of unity or similarities within the group	**Examples of diversity or differences within the group**
Examples of the unity or similarities within the class	**Examples of diversity or differences within the class**

Our group proposes that the following goals and values define our national unity:
_____
_____
_____
_____

The symbol our group will develop is:
_____

This symbol reflects the national identity of our class in the following ways:
_____
_____
_____
_____

HISTORY SIMULATION 35

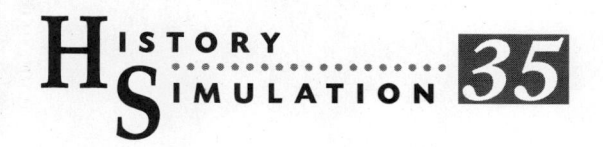

Give Peace a Chance

There have been many efforts to bring peace to the Middle East since 1945. Most people in the Middle East want peace—as long as certain conditions are met. As you have seen in this chapter, the stability or lack of stability of the Middle East affects many countries outside the region, including the United States. The United States and other countries have worked with the leaders of several Middle Eastern nations to try to resolve the problems of that region.

TEACHER MATERIAL

Learning Objective To practice negotiation and mediation skills in conflict resolution.

Activity Students simulate organizing and conducting a peace negotiation.

Teacher Preparation Make one copy of the handout material for each student.

Activity Guidelines

1. Review Chapter 35 with students. Discuss the issues that concern the different parties involved in the ongoing Israeli-Palestinian conflict. Point out that much progress has been made, yet as events such as the assassination of Yitzhak Rabin and the suicide bombings of early 1996 have shown, the progress might be characterized as two steps forward and one step back.

2. Invite students to choose one of the major issues that still need to be resolved in the Israeli-Palestinian conflict. These may be selected from pages 962–963 of the textbook, or from issues currently in the news.

3. As a class, determine which parties have an interest in the resolution of the issue chosen. (For example, if the issue is troops in Lebanon, the parties involved include Syria, Israel, Lebanon, the PLO.) Discuss the issues that concern each party and how it relates to the conflict.

4. Organize the class into groups representing the parties to the conflict, plus one or two mediating groups. Have the groups draw lots to determine which group will play which party or mediator in the conflict.

5. When the groups have their assignments, they will discuss the concerns of their group in the conflict. Students should do additional research to learn more about the history of the conflict as it has affected their group. Students in a mediator group will try to inform themselves as broadly as possible about the conflict as a whole. Remind students in these groups that they are mediators, not judges. Their job is to help the parties in the conflict find a solution, not to decide themselves what is right or wrong. After each group has finished its research, the members will fill out the top half of the handout material.

6. Each group will select one or two members to represent them at the peace conference. Mediators will facilitate the conference and try to lead members of the other parties toward a resolution.

7. When a resolution has been proposed and accepted by the parties at the conference, representatives will return to their groups and inform them of the conference resolution. Members of the groups will express their approval or disapproval of the resolution. The resolution and reactions to it should be recorded on the bottom of the handout.

8. The whole class will discuss the success or failure of the conference. Students should realize that if some groups are extremely unhappy with the resolution, they might engage in boycotts, embargoes, terrorism, or warfare to change the outcome. Ask students to predict how successful they think their negotiations will be in increasing stability in the Middle East.

Name .... Date .... Class ....

History Simulation 35

HANDOUT MATERIAL

Give Peace a Chance Worksheet

Group _____

Representative #1 _____ **Representative #2** _____

Concerns	
Past Events	
Allies	
Opponents	

Resolution _____

Reaction _____

Predicted Outcome _____

HISTORY SIMULATION 36

Name That Leader

Much of Chapter 36 profiles the succession of Latin American leaders—charismatic, dictatorial, progressive—since World War II and traces their successes and failures. The following activity is designed to reinforce the names and roles of these leaders.

TEACHER MATERIAL

Learning Objective To demonstrate how Latin American leaders between World War II and the present attempted to solve national and hemispheric problems.

Activity Individual students will assume the identities of various Latin American leaders discussed in Chapter 36. The class will form three teams and ask one another a series of yes/no questions to discover the identity of each leader.

Teacher Preparation Make one copy of the handout on page 72 for each student.

Activity Guidelines

1. Introduce the activity to students by explaining its objective and general steps.

2. Organize the class into three teams, one for each region discussed in Chapter 36: Mexico and the Caribbean, Central America, and South America. Then have each group choose a timekeeper, a scorekeeper, and a host. These positions will rotate so that every student gets to participate.

3. Tell the groups to choose three or more political leaders of their region. (Check students' lists to make sure that the leaders were, in fact, important within that region and eliminate any who were not.) Next tell them to decide which students will represent which leaders on a panel. Students who are not on the panel will serve as press secretaries for the leaders, assisting them with specific dates or facts if panelists can't remember. (Press secretaries will be allowed to refer to their textbooks.) Tell the timekeeper to allow 10 minutes for groups to make their selections.

4. To begin play, select one team to function as the panel of leaders. The host should announce which region is being featured. Then members from the other two teams alternate asking yes/no questions of one panelist at a time. Only 10 questions can be asked of any one panelist. If a team member correctly identifies the political leader on the first try, 10 points are earned. On the second try, 9 points are earned, and so on. If the political leader is not correctly identified, the group of panelists earns 10 points. If a team member asks a question that cannot be answered yes or no, then that team loses 1 point and forfeits the play. Tell the timekeeper to allow only 10 minutes for each group of panelists. If the group of panelists runs out of leaders before the time is up, then each team asking questions earns an extra 10 points.

5. Just before the end of class, ask students which leaders or events they found difficult to identify or discuss. Encourage students to review pertinent sections of the chapter before the chapter test is administered.

Name .... Date .... Class ....

History Simulation 36

HANDOUT MATERIAL

Name That Leader

Check the box next to your group's region.

☐ Mexico and the Caribbean   ☐ Central America   ☐ South America

List the leaders who will be on your group's panel and write biographical notes about each one.

Leaders	Notes

List any questions you want to ask panelists from other regions.

_____
_____
_____

Leaders and/or events you need to review:

_____
_____
_____

72   History Simulations   World History

HISTORY SIMULATION 37

Cash for Your Country

As nations become increasingly interdependent, they must seek new ways to cooperate. Since World War II, many developing nations have worked to improve their economies and standards of living. The World Bank and International Monetary Fund have made many loans to countries that are trying to make improvements.

TEACHER MATERIAL

Learning Objective To demonstrate the need for cooperation among nations.

Activity An international body has announced that $1 million will be given to any country that can justify the need for it. Each group of students, representing an assigned country, will present its case before the international body.

Teacher Preparation Make a copy of the worksheet on the next page for each student.

Activity Guidelines

1. Introduce the activity by reviewing the concept of cooperation. Ask students to cite specific instances of international cooperation from their textbooks (arms control, the European Union, the Montreal Protocol).

2. Tell students that they will demonstrate the need for international cooperation by preparing a proposal to submit to an international body that has announced grants of $1 million to any country that can prove its need. Further explain that the countries that make proposals should consider long-term, self-help measures as well as measures to meet immediate problems the money might help to solve. For example, a country might propose that part of the money be spent to import emergency food—an example of meeting immediate needs—and that other portions of the money be spent to develop resources, reclaim farmland, and promote family planning.

3. Organize the class into four groups and distribute the worksheets. Assign each group one of the numbered countries. Tell group members to decide on a name for their country and to choose the following tasks: group leader, recorder, budget committee, proposal writer, and presenter.

4. Have students proceed as follows:
   a. Group members have 5 minutes to study the situation described on the worksheet.
   b. The group discusses the situation and decides on the needs of the country. The recorder writes them on the worksheet.
   c. A plan of action is discussed and a consensus reached. The plan is written on the worksheet by the recorder, who then gives the worksheet to the budget committee.
   d. The committee proposes budget allocations for the plans. A member records the budget on the worksheet and gives it to the writer.
   e. The writer prepares a persuasive proposal to be made before the international body.
   f. Have the presenter rehearse the proposal before his or her own group. Then he or she makes the proposal before the international body (the remainder of the class).

5. After each country has made its proposal, have students discuss all of them. Then have them vote on which country they feel is entitled to a grant. (All countries may be awarded a grant.)

6. Following the vote, discuss the activity. Some questions you may want to ask include:
   - Why did you approve the country or countries that you did?
   - Why did you disapprove the countries (if any) that you did?
   - How did the countries' proposals demonstrate the need for cooperation?

Name _____ Date _____ Class _____

HISTORY SIMULATION 37

HANDOUT MATERIAL

Aid Application

Group Leader _____ Recorder _____ Presenter _____
Proposal Writer _____ Budget Committee _____

Country 1 Has always raised most of its own food. However, the population is growing rapidly, and recent natural disasters have cut farm production in half. As a result, famine threatens. A rare ore has been discovered that could turn the economy around. However, the country has resisted efforts from multinational corporations to develop mining.

Country 2 Has been developing rapidly in the past 10 years. Heavily populated, it is attractive to multinational corporations as a source of inexpensive labor. Although the country has had a primarily agricultural economy, many people have moved into the cities to work. Cities are becoming overcrowded and the capital is experiencing an outbreak of cholera. In order to attract more industry to provide more jobs and have enough money to provide basic services for increasing numbers of city dwellers, a cheap source of energy is available.

Country 3 This island nation has always depended on its export of tropical fruit to survive. However, rapid population growth has caused the country to experience economic problems. Its income from exports has not matched the amount needed to import food. Because of an inadequate, unbalanced diet, many people are malnourished. The only resource the country has, other than fruit growing, is its natural beauty.

Country 4 This country has recently gained its independence from another nation that had largely supplied its economic needs and exploited its natural resources. The population is largely uneducated and does not possess the technological skills necessary to operate the industry established by the mother country. Basic needs of the people are not being met, unemployment is high, and there is political unrest.

Country # _____ Name of Country _____

Needs   Plan   Budget
_____   _____   _____
_____   _____   _____
_____   _____   _____
_____   _____   _____
_____   _____   _____
_____   _____   _____
_____   _____   _____
_____   _____   _____

Teacher's Notes

Teacher's Notes